C000228498

– The –
FOREVER AN

"P. M. H. Atwater, in her new study, establishes that the full pattern of NDE aftereffects—physical, mental, emotional, spiritual—has a far greater impact on children (and adults) than anyone thought or has found before. She concludes that it takes the average child experiencer at least twenty to forty years to integrate their NDE, because they usually try to compensate, to adjust, and to ignore. This new book is a very important and valuable contribution to our knowledge and insight about NDE in very young children."
PIM VAN LOMMEL, M.D., NDE RESEARCHER AND
AUTHOR OF *CONSCIOUSNESS BEYOND LIFE*

"In *The Forever Angels,* P. M. H. Atwater tackles the particular challenges of the very youngest near-death experiencers but from an innovative angle. In this novel approach, Atwater interviewed hundreds of people near the end of life who recalled having had an NDE in their first years of life. This strategy gives us an unprecedented "long view" of how NDEs influence these children over the entire course of their lives. Unlike adult experiencers, these children did not have the chance to develop "normal" attitudes and behavior patterns before their NDEs, which makes them a unique group of people, with unique traits and challenges. There is no other book like this, nor is there likely to be one."
BRUCE GREYSON, M.D., CARLSON PROFESSOR EMERITUS OF
PSYCHIATRY AND NEUROBEHAVIORAL SCIENCES
AT THE UNIVERSITY OF VIRGINIA HEALTH SYSTEM

"In her truly groundbreaking book, P. M. H. Atwater has boldly gone where no researcher has dared to go before—into the lives of the newly born who have had NDEs. And what she has found gives us an important new way to view NDEs—for these children, it isn't what we thought. P. M. H. Atwater is the field's most creative and tireless researcher! This is a helluva book."
KENNETH RING, PH.D., AUTHOR OF *LESSONS FROM THE LIGHT:
WHAT WE CAN LEARN FROM THE NEAR-DEATH EXPERIENCE*

"I had a near-death experience when I was five years old, and I had not understood my early childhood difficulties until I read *The Forever Angels.*

Besides helping you understand yourself, this book's greatest value may be for parents who need to understand an alienated child, a child in great need of finding security at home."

BARBARA HAND CLOW, AUTHOR OF *THE MIND CHRONICLES: A VISIONARY GUIDE INTO PAST LIVES*

"One of the most influential researchers into the mystery of the near-death experience is P. M. H. Atwater. She has given a voice to those whose experiences during childhood and infancy has, to date, been somewhat neglected and, in doing so, has given other authors like myself, a great deal of food for thought and an intriguing new area of investigation."

ANTHONY PEAKE, AUTHOR OF *OPENING THE DOORS OF PERCEPTION*

"P. M. H. Atwater is unafraid to venture into sketchily charted territory. Using her considerable knowledge and skills, in direct staccato style, she exposes life experiences too fragile or too subliminal for others to have unmasked. Read *The Forever Angels*; you will be guided beyond the mundane into our larger existence."

LYNN B. ROBINSON, PH.D., AUTHOR OF *LOVING TO THE END . . . AND ON*

"If you want to know what really happens in near-death and out-of-body experiences in the words of real people in the real world, look no further. P. M. H. Atwater has assembled an astonishing collection of accounts that shows us not only what occurs during these events but how they impact the individual's development over the lifespan. A beautiful work!"

REV. TERRI DANIEL, M.A., CT, END-OF-LIFE ADVISOR, INTERFAITH CHAPLAIN, AND FOUNDER OF THE AFTERLIFE CONFERENCE

"As a psychotherapist, I found this book expanded my understanding of the powerful impact of NDEs on children's development. I recommend this very readable, very interesting book. It's full of detailed information that will be especially relevant for psychotherapists working with young children."

FONYA LORD HELM, PH.D., ABPP

"*The Forever Angels* is a triumph. I was riveted from beginning to end with these amazing stories. "

JULIE LOAR, AWARD-WINNING AUTHOR OF *GODDESSES FOR EVERY DAY*

"A fascinating review of the youngest survivors of near-death experiences."

KAREN NEWELL, COAUTHOR *LIVING IN A MINDFUL UNIVERSE*

– The –
FOREVER
ANGELS

Near-Death Experiences in Childhood and Their Lifelong Impact

P. M. H. Atwater, L.H.D.

Bear & Company
Rochester, Vermont

Bear & Company
One Park Street
Rochester, Vermont 05767
www.BearandCompanyBooks.com

Text stock is SFI certified

Bear & Company is a division of Inner Traditions International

Cataloging-in-Publication Data for this title is available from the Library of Congress

ISBN 978-1-59143-358-3 (print)
ISBN 978-1-59143-359-0 (ebook)

Printed and bound in the United States by Lake Book Manufacturing, Inc.
The text stock is SFI certified. The Sustainable Forestry Initiative® program
promotes sustainable forest management.

10 9 8 7 6 5 4 3 2 1

Text design by Priscilla Baker and layout by Debbie Glogover
This book was typeset in Garamond Premier Pro with Acherus Grotesque and
Futura Std used as display tyepfaces

To send correspondence to the author of this book, mail a first-class letter to the
author c/o Inner Traditions • Bear & Company, One Park Street, Rochester, VT
05767, and we will forward the communication, or contact the author directly at
www.pmhatwater.com.

This book is dedicated to Tracy Coen.

Her near-death experience occurred in utero while her mother was attempting suicide. Memories of both her episode and its aftereffects became a lifelong journey into the very heart of her soul. She was very anxious to read the results of this study but died before it could be finished.

We all miss you, Tracy.

Living life from a child experiencer perspective has been quite challenging. As a child, when you feel other people's suffering and emotions, have little or no say in things, feel duty bound to help others and that you can handle the extra burdens . . . life doesn't feel safe. It's hard to be here. Contrary to the ecstasy most adult experiencers have from their NDE, a child has to try to manage being in this world— and manage their "gifts" and sensitivities. I've spent almost my entire life not wanting to be here. Knowing oneness (in some fashion), all sentient beings are treated with respect and their journey is sacred. Often, I have been put in a position to say a harsh word or step up to negative behavior. It gets very tiring. Earth is very harsh and I often long for the refinement of the other side. It's easier to breathe there. The only way I've learned and dared to investigate my own feelings has been through talking with child experiencers I trust. Physical life is very small for me but my internal life is expansive. It is fascinating and difficult. Child experiencers have a great deal to share when viewed from another perspective.

CARA (CASE 14). SHE DIED BETWEEN
THREE AND A HALF AND FOUR YEARS OF AGE
DURING A TONSILLECTOMY. EMERGENCY MEASURES
WERE TAKEN TO SAVE HER.

Contents

Child Experiencers
Are Different

A newspaper headline of March 2015 reads: "Toddler Dead for 101 Minutes Is Now Alive." The news clip told of a Pennsylvania toddler who was pulled from an icy creek. No pulse. No breathing. No neurological function. Yet the child came back to life—unscathed.

Death of the very young seems somehow obscene, as if in all certainty such a thing must be a violation of God's will. Their stories grab us, and we hang on every detail, every word said. Yet once the full story is revealed, folks backstep . . . because in 70 to 80 percent of the cases, either of a near-miss, terrible fright, or total finality, the children who survive talk about what it was like to be quite alive on the other side of death . . . wide-awake alive in their mother's womb . . . totally alive in worlds beyond this one. They describe what is called a "near-death experience," or NDE. (Note that these terms are used interchangeably throughout the text.)

For the record, a near-death experience is generally described as an intense awareness, sense, or experience of otherworldliness, whether pleasant or unpleasant, that happens to people at the edge of death. It is of such magnitude that most experiencers are deeply affected—many to the point of making significant changes in their life afterward. Medical research affirms that while clinically dead, close to death, or in a state of utter shock (a fear death), an individual can have a vivid out-of-body experience, clear enhanced consciousness, self-identity with emotions, cognition—thought perception, full use of faculties, intact memories—*all of this happening when the brain is NOT working, nor are heart and lungs*.[1] There are cases where individuals revived in the morgue, much to the shock of morgue personnel.*

I entered this research field in 1978, the year after I was raped and had experienced crisis after crisis that resulted in death/near death three times in three months and later, a total collapse, body systems barely functioning, my blood pressure at 60/60. Along with having to relearn everything from the ground up, what turned my world upside down was not only what I witnessed "elsewhere" but also a voice "bigger than big" that spoke to me during my third episode, saying, "Test revelation. You are to do the research. One book for each death." I was shown what that meant but not how to do the work. The first book was not named by The Voice at the time, but the second and third were.[2]

The way I was raised as a child determined "how I did what I did." Yup, I was a cop's kid raised in a police station (went there often for a ride home during Dad's coffee breaks). Dad always said, "The body says more than the mouth does," which means you don't just ask questions of people, you observe their every movement. Body language can be quite "loud" sometimes. And you involve significant others—neighbors, spouses, children, caregivers, whoever will talk to you—and have sessions with them, too. I shy away from "scientific protocols" because they

*The most famous of these is the case of George Rodonaia, a Communist dissident, living in Tbilisi, Georgia. He was run down by a taxi driven by KGB agents and rushed to the hospital where he was dead on arrival. His corpse was put in a morgue freezer vault where it remained for three days before being pulled out for autopsy. He revived during autopsy. His case is discussed in two of my books: *Beyond the Light* (still available through the Amazon website) and *The Big Book of Near-Death Experiences,* available through Rainbow Ridge Books, the International Association for Near-Death Studies, and/or Amazon.

are biased (use words before the individual does) and do not dig deep enough, nor are they thorough (at least not thorough enough for me).

There's not a single skeptic I know of, in regard to near-death research, who has done original work with experiencers of any import or verified what they found by enlarging their study to involve experiencers in other areas and differing ages and intents, races, or religions. Nor have they always taken care not to "lead" anyone or to be ever alert to aftereffects and any pattern that might follow. Call me a snoop if you want. Just know I have been doing this—everything original—for forty years and involving nearly 5,000 adult and child experiencers, either personally or by phone, letter, or emails.[3]

This book is the second I've tackled on the subject of what happens to kids and what they have to say. The first was in the late nineties involving 277 children with experiences that occurred between the womb and fifteen years of age. It is chronicled in *The New Children and Near-Death Experiences.** With this newest project, I've gone after "the long view" once they had fully matured—what was it like while young with Mom and Dad, siblings, friends, school, dating, sex, growing up, jobs, marriage, handling money, spirituality, religion, personal views.

The three basic human drives that propel all of humankind are identity, community, and purpose. What happens to children who grow up with an entirely different view of these three concepts? What happens to those with womb memory and of other worlds beyond this one? What happens to those who clearly and in detail remember their

---

*My first try reporting my findings with child experiencers of near-death states was heavily edited and redesigned by my publisher, Three Rivers Press. They also renamed the book *Children of the New Millennium.* Nearly two-thirds of my research was deleted in this process. In 2003, Bear & Co., an imprint of Inner Traditions, allowed me to resurrect this material in *The New Children and Near-Death Experiences,* which exists today as an intensive study of what happens to children who undergo the phenomenon. An additional feature in this second version is a comparison between near-death kids and the "new kids" (those born since 1982). The similarities between them are further explored in *Children of the Fifth World.*

birth? What happens to the youngest of the young who know, absolutely *know,* their parents are not their parents—that they belong elsewhere? What happens when tiny ones bond to the other side—NOT with their parents—or don't fit in with siblings? What happens when the innocent know more, feel more, see more, remember more than any child could or should?

Child experiencers of near-death states are not like adult experiencers. Most cannot compare "before" with "after" as adults do, *because they don't have a "before"*—at least not in this world. They emerge as outliers, called upon to create and invent unique ways of living and loving. Dr. Penny Sartori, in her runaway bestseller *The Wisdom of Near-Death Experiences,*[4] says these children lead charmed lives afterward. Indeed they do, once they figure out how to balance worlds within worlds. Stories of the smallest experiencers of the near-death phenomenon are both inspiring and troubling. Because of this, we're taking a deep plunge in this book—to shine light on the whole picture—what we want to see and what we don't, what can be verified and what cannot.

My thanks to Beverly Brodsky, Stephanie Wiltse, Bill Guggenheim, Diane Corcoran, staff and volunteers at the International Association for Near-Death Studies, and Linda Layne, my editor. All of you helped me so much that I feel as if this book is as much yours as mine. And thanks to the Internet: once you put a request "out there," it just keeps going and going until enough people finally step forward and say, *Me too!*

It's taken several decades for the various stages of this project to be completed. I can now stack this one atop the first and say with full voice: *Children have more to show us than anyone ever imagined.*

Jan's (case 7) earliest memories: "As a toddler, I often 'dreamed' of my older and younger brothers. My older brother had died before he was born. It was not the time for my younger brother to be conceived. Conceptually, as a toddler, I could not understand where either one of

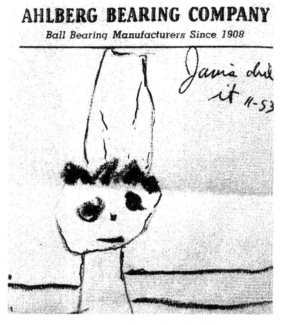

Jan remembers her birth,
drawing done when a toddler

them were when I woke up each morning. I would see my older brother, John, at the foot of my bed before I went to sleep and sometimes, he and my younger brother were with me when I slept. I spent many mornings looking all over the house for the two of them, followed by many questions to Mom about where they were. Later I found out Mom had a miscarriage before my older sister was born. The baby had been a boy they had named John. This was verification of who I had seen. I was told I went through this 'annoying' behavior of looking for my brothers for several years before my baby brother was actually conceived and born. I stopped asking where John was after my little brother arrived. After that, John did not come to mind anymore, although there were several visits from him in my sleep. John told me his job was supposed to have been to protect me and my sister. He said he would have to do so from his spirit form and not in a bodily form."

ONE

What's Here

I am on a journey toward God and am not afraid of death
for I have been shown what to expect.

JACK (CASE 101)

*T*he standard scenario for a near-death experience forms around these elements: ineffability (beyond the limits of any language to describe), hearing yourself pronounced dead, feelings of peace and quiet, hearing unusual noises, seeing a dark tunnel, finding yourself outside your body, meeting "spiritual beings," a very bright light experienced as a "being of light," a panoramic life review, sensing a border or limit to where you can go, coming back to your body, frustrating attempts to tell others about what happened to you, subtle "broadening and deepening" of your life afterward, elimination of the fear of death, and corroboration of events witnessed while out of your body. Also reported: a realm where all knowledge exists, cities of light, a realm of bewildered spirits, and supernatural rescues.

Sorry, but this standard doesn't always fit, especially with the young. If you factor in emotions, before and after events and responses, including the pattern of aftereffects, what you find instead are "experience types"—four of them: initial experience, unpleasant or hell-like experience, pleasant or heaven-like experience, and transcendent experience.

It's as if the experiencer's own consciousness—on some level—has a pre-dominate part to play in what occurs . . . and perhaps why.

What I discovered about the four types follows. Note that the statistics are based on 3,000 adult and 277 child experiencers of near-death states.

Initial experience—sometimes referred to as the "nonexperience" (an awakening). This involves only one or maybe a couple of elements, such as a loving nothingness, the living dark, a friendly voice, a brief out-of-body experience, or a manifestation of some type. It is usually experienced by those who seem to need the least amount of evidence for proof of survival, or who need the least amount of shake-up in their lives at that point in time. Often, this becomes a "seed" experience or an introduction to other ways of perceiving and recognizing reality. Rarely is any other element present. Incident rate: 76 percent with child experiencers, 20 percent with adult experiencers.

Unpleasant or hell-like experience—sometimes referred to as "distressing" (inner cleansing and self-confrontational). This is an encounter with a threatening void, stark limbo, or hellish purgatory, or scenes of a startling and unexpected indifference (like being shunned) or even "hauntings" from one's own past. These scenarios are usually experienced by those who seem to have deeply suppressed or repressed guilt, fear, and anger or those who expect some kind of punishment or discomfort after death. Life reviews are common. Some have life previews. Incident rate: 3 percent with child experiencers, 15 percent with adult experiencers.

Pleasant or heaven-like experience—sometimes referred to as "radiant" (reassurance and self-validation). This is a heaven-like scenario of loving family reunions with those who have died previously, reassuring religious figures or light beings, validation that life counts, or affirmative and inspiring dialogue. These scenarios are usually experienced by those who most need to know how loved they are and how important life is and how every effort has a purpose in the overall scheme of things. Life reviews are common. Some have life previews. Incident rate: 19 percent with child experiencers, 47 percent with adult experiencers.

Transcendent experience—sometimes referred to as "collective universality" (expansive revelations, alternate realities). This type involves exposure to otherworldly dimensions and scenes beyond the individual's frame of reference and sometimes includes revelations of greater truths. Seldom personal in content, the scenarios are usually experienced by those who are ready for a "mind stretching" challenge or individuals who are more apt to use, to whatever degree, the truths that are revealed to them. Life reviews are rare. Collective previews (the world's future, evolutionary changes, etc.) are common. Incident rate: 2 percent with child experiencers, 18 percent with adult experiencers.

Hands down, more children have the initial experience than any other type. Why might that be? They simply don't need the extra drama.

Then there's that business with tunnels. In 1982, the Gallup Poll did the first-ever scientific survey on the subject. Only 9 percent of the people reported a tunnel. Today, tunnel reports average around one-fourth to one-third of known cases. And, that's mostly in the United States plus a few other countries. Typically, experiencers, no matter where in the world they are, hardly ever mention them. Yes, adults and children do report tunnels, yet, not that many. Scenes of hospital surgical rooms, beeping machinery, and nurses and doctors running around doesn't fit either, since only between 12 to 27 percent of near-death cases ever happen in a hospital setting.

So where on earth is this "light at the end of the tunnel" stuff coming from? The media.

You can trace it back to where it all began . . . when the media was trying to sensationalize Dr. Raymond Moody's classic, *Life after Life.*[1] Why they did this is pretty obvious: money (sponsors buy the most advertising from sensational broadcasts and shows), and time (if you don't grab viewers quick you lose them). Thus, what was true for the few became true for the many, even when it wasn't.

Another surprise: the *living* occasionally show up in children's episodes. I've found this with adults, too, but mostly with kids. Over the years I've observed that living "visitors"—maybe a friend next door, a favorite teacher, someone trusted—serve as "comforters" and these special folks remain visible only as long as it takes to "steady" the child and dispel fear, then they disappear, and elements more typical of near-death states follow.

Only once did I find a *mutually remembered visitation* between the one who died and the living one who gave aid, and it was with adults. The man who left his body in death "called out" to a friend for help. She "appeared" just long enough to ease his fears, then disappeared. Years later the two saw each other at a meeting I was hosting. He asked if she remembered helping him then. She did. What she remembered, though, was dreaming he called out to her and her response. The dream she had turned out to be "more than real."

Typical as well with kids is what happened to Jan (case 7). You just saw her drawing and read about her experience at the end of the introduction. When old enough to talk, she was regularly visited by the dead *and* the unborn: an older brother her mother had previously miscarried and a younger brother not yet conceived. Also, being aware of, or maybe even having a relationship with, a twin who was reabsorbed back into the mother's body early in the pregnancy is fairly common. Called "the missing twin phenomenon,"* Elvis Presley, the famous singer/actor, regularly conversed with his twin brother who had died before he was born.

Stories about aborted babies, missing twins, the appearance of relatives who died before the child was born, meeting in childhood the very children the experiencer will one day parent once grown, life in worlds beyond this one . . . ah, if you think any of this is beyond belief—just wait.

---

*Raymond W. Brandt, Ph.D. published both *Twins World Magazine* and *Twinless Twins Newsletter* until his death in 2001. His board of directors is continuing his work. To obtain either or both of these publications, plus information about support groups and regional gatherings, contact Twinless Twins Support Group (see "Resources").

TWO

Who's Here

NDErs on stage, on TV—none came from poverty. How about NDEs with the poor?

JOYCE (CASE 110)

*T*he original work I did surprised just about everyone because the only other research with children available at the time was done by Melvin Morse, M.D. (author of *Closer to the Light*) in the United States and Cherie Sutherland (author of *Children of the Light*) in Australia/New Zealand. My goal then was to see if those with womb and birth memories, babies and toddlers on up to teenagers, followed the same near-death and aftereffects patterning as do adults. I was looking for "markers," or significant details that could signal causal realities. I found plenty of them.

The following list is a spread of those who participated in my first study:

- 60 percent White—United States, Canada, England, France, England, Ukraine
- 23 percent Latino—United States, Mexico, Argentina, Colombia
- 12 percent Black—United States, Canada
- 5 percent Asian—Malaysia, China

Parents were interviewed too, as I wanted their point of view and whether they may have applied any pressure on their child, as kids are quite capable of slanting their stories to fit the emotional expectations of their parents and/or teachers. I rejected 15 percent of the interview opportunities I had with kids for this reason. When working with little ones, the pupils of your eyes can never be above theirs. This establishes genuine interest and trust. You guessed it: if they were small, I spent most of my time on the floor with them, sometimes on my belly.

I quickly learned that although adults and children displayed similar patterning with scenarios and aftereffects, they were worlds apart in how the phenomenon affected them at both the moment of *and* over time.

Here's the typical process of development for children up to fifteen years old: Birth to fifteen months is when the actual wiring of the brain is determined and synapse formation increases twentyfold. This process utilizes twice the energy of an adult brain. Between three and five years old is the time of temporal lobe development, where the child explores and experiments with possible roles, future patterns, and the continuity of their environment. Ten to fifteen years old is puberty time with lots of hormone fluctuations, questions about sexuality, and crises of identity.

Amazingly, my largest cluster of cases was between three to five years of age; the second largest was from birth to fifteen months. Drowning was the major cause of death/near-death, followed by such crises as birth complications, high fever, surgery, accidents, and child abuse. That largest cluster—three to five years of age—is the exact time when most healthy children see, engage with, and report alien abductions, fairy sightings, monsters, and angel visitations. The birth to fifteen months group is where I found the strongest evidence of the presence of genius—without genetic markers to account for it.

Now do you understand why I wanted to study child experiencers one more time? There're just too many anomalies and not enough people asking why. To accomplish this task, I turned the scenery around. "Write me your story," I said. And I asked these simple questions to crowds of people: "Did any of you have a near-death experience or something like it—when you were born, a baby, a toddler, or anytime up to five years old? Do you have any womb memories or any verification?" I asked open-ended questions on a flier: "What was it like with Mom and Dad afterward and with siblings, friends, school, sex, relationships, jobs, living in the world, your health, or becoming a parent? Did you have any therapy or problems with alcohol/drugs?" Basically, what I wanted was an essay. What I got was an outpouring from people finally freed to say whatever they wanted. No strings. One man was so thrilled to tell his story he sent me page after page after page, a virtual book complete with photographs. Several submissions were so tearstained I could hardly read them. One woman on food stamps pinched enough pennies to buy the stamps she needed to mail me her submission. And she wasn't the only one who spoke from the depths of poverty and depression—smiling because someone cared enough to ask.

These 120 people bared their souls. Here's the breakdown of who they were: thirty-four were men, eighty-six were women; the oldest was eighty-six, the youngest was twenty-one, and the majority were middle-aged; half were retired or not working, the other half had jobs, three were in college. One was a Catholic sister and another was a county commissioner. There was also a man who was once nominated for a Nobel Peace Prize. Several were twins, and each twin was involved in the same/mutual near-death scenario.

Their ethnic makeup was as follows: three African Americans, four Asians (Japan and Sri Lanka), three Hispanics (South America), five Native Americans (various tribal nations), one Inuit, one Aborigine, one Basque, seventy-six Whites (America, Canada, Northern Territories), and twenty-six additional Whites (from South Africa, England, Australia, Netherlands, Italy, what was once the Soviet Zone/Germany, Ireland, Iceland, Sweden, Greece, Poland, Israel).

Of these people, one was legally blind, one had cerebral palsy, one was autistic, three came from families that practice voodoo, and one claimed to be a double walk-in (a phenomenon reportedly where one soul leaves a given body for whatever reason while another soul comes in to take the original's place—in this case the claim was that the soul exchange occurred twice over a span of several decades).

The death/womb/birth event breakdown went like this: thirty-three had womb memories, thirty-three remembered their birth, twenty-one were infants/toddlers, six had an NDE between the ages of one and one and a half years, six had an NDE between two and two and a half years, seventeen had their episode between three and three and a half years, twelve had one between four and four and a half years, and fourteen had one at five years. Two claimed alien abduction, six had dark light scenarios (as will be defined later), one had a clear light experience, and another reported a soul merge with an alien. There were two cases of missing twins who were reunited, three cases that were connected with sexual abuse, and two who were used by their parents for demonic rituals (one of those born into a cult had seventeen near-death experiences while still small, the first occurred when she was six weeks old—it's a miracle she is still alive). This adds up to 177 events. Obviously, some had multiple experiences before age six.

An additional three are not part of this count. Though they died at birth and were immediately resuscitated, none remember anything in particular about it, nor do they exhibit unique aftereffects. Studying them and the way they lived their life afterward was helpful in my search for markers that could prove meaningful. Other cases are pulled in from other studies when fitting.

As you can readily see, the volunteers in this study are all over the map. Their experiences are just as varied as where they live, how they live, and who they are. The canvas of their childhood, however, reveals something rather startling: *all of them remember living before their birth and being quite alive after their death.*

THREE

In Their Own Words

Our stories belong to each other.

CLOTHILDE (CASE 57)

Glee (case 105), intensive care, hospital in the Philippines. NDE at age five from whooping cough. "I remember going up below the clouds. As I was ascending, I heard children laugh and play, but when I went above the clouds, I did not see any kids. I was on clouds. Everything was white around me. The only colors I saw were Mylar balloons with strings, standing on clouds. Then on the side of me, I catch a glimpse of 3 male figures in their 60s or 70s. They had long white gowns, like Jesus Christ, back then. Their gowns were glowing . . . not exactly solid. They had grey/white hair (not a lot of hair) and white, short trim beard. They did not speak to me, but I also did not feel threatened by them. I recall communication with a higher power, 'though I did not see. I felt the presence. I was communicating telepathically. All of a sudden my surrounding turned pitch dark. I was in the universe. I recall a few stars here and there. So tiny, I didn't know what they were, but there was one dot I saw and it kept coming closer and closer, it was planet earth. I got to see the landscape as it was turning, like it is now. But one thing that made me want to come back was the life experiences from the billions of people on earth. I was able to feel what they went through in an instant and was able to feel each individual's life or their emotional experiences. It was amazing and intriguing and I asked to come back and so, here I am. I couldn't talk about this. No one would believe me."

Carmen (case 11), off the coast Spain. NDE at age four, saw a "business angel" in the clouds on the way to school with her father, presaged her drowning soon after.

Mimi (case 117). NDE at age one and a half, vicious beating from father. "My father was angry at me. He shouted at me and took me two stairs up to the attic where my bed was. He stripped me till I was completely naked and started to beat me with one of the 'English books,'

Carmen, NDE at age four

beautiful books with dazzling drawings. While he was doing that I lost consciousness. The pain was unbearable and the next moment I found myself in a huge tunnel. With great speed I was moving through space, higher and higher. SUPER FAST!!! It took a long time. An annoying noise surrounded me. All of a sudden I saw a light in the distance. The attractive power of this light was irresistible. I don't know if I was afraid but it was extremely unpleasant with a nasty sound in the tunnel. The light came closer until I stood in dazzling bright light. It felt very comfortable, perfect temperature, nourishing. The definition 'COMING HOME' is the closest. I saw an enormous shiny entrance gate. In the gateway stood a LIGHT BEING (male). This BEING reacted friendly. Without words there was instant understanding. Immediately I was surrounded by 4 or 5 light beings and was told to choose between righteousness and unrighteousness. These concepts were written in huge letters over a crazy big rainbow. The biggest rainbow you can imagine. They were in a language not seen in this world, sort of a living Alphabet, a secret language of signs!!! The signs began to live. I got complete information in 6D. It was like a multidimensional reality. Sort of like a library which you can visit from all dimensions. Time, space, consequences, and effects on others or the environment, wavelength, frequency, holy geometry. In one second I was aware of the meaning of this for the world. The light being spoke to me: 'Now you know, you have a job to fulfill. You have to go back to earth.' I was 1½ years old and could not speak yet. Nevertheless, I carry the knowledge inside of me as if it is normal."

Damon (case 112). NDE at age three, drowning. "I don't recall entering the water but I keenly remember the sudden sense of darkness and swirling sandy water around my face. I remember feeling calm, as though all would be ok. The next bit is where it became strange. I'm staring at a little boy who is standing crying, arms raised slightly from his side, watching the sand and water run off him (see drawing). I'm up close to his face and I'm amazed and amused by the sight of sand

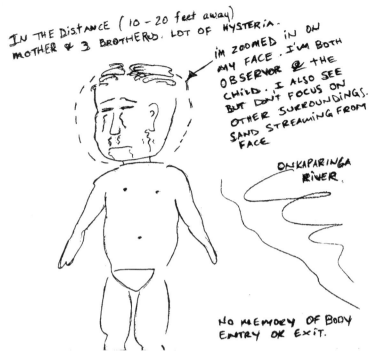

Damon, NDE at age three

running from eyes, ears, and nose. The thought goes through my mind, *I didn't know so much sand could come from a boy's nose, eyes, and ears.* There's no compassion or empathy, to me it's all fine and nothing to carry on about. To my left (the toddler's right), I can hear my mother hysterical, the toddler is crying, and there's a commotion over what has just happened. I have little patience for it. It goes through my mind: *What's all the silly noise about, calm down, nothing dramatic has happened.* I knew the child was me and who everyone was, although I felt no real attachment to any of them."

Jack (case 101). NDE at age three, ten-foot fall over protective railing. "I was in the attic with my mother. I can remember very clearly every detail. I was walking around holding my pillow. I loved to feel the soft fabric and was holding the pillow in front of me. The next thing I remember is being up in a large tree in our front yard next to the walk, and watching my mother run out of our house toward our next-door neighbor's house. I wondered what she was carrying in her arms. Then I realized it was me. I wasn't concerned. I just watched. The next thing I remember is being slammed down and water running over my face. I opened my eyes and saw that I was on the countertop with my head in the sink. My mother told me later that I fell over the protective railing around the steps and landed on the steps some 10 feet below. For years I never told anyone about my experience. One thing that puzzled me about this fall was the tree I was in while my mother ran next door. We didn't have a tree in our front yard next to the walk. I remember later, when my father wanted to plant a tree, he asked where we thought would be the best place. I immediately responded and was very determined that the tree be planted next to the walk. I was so insistent that he planted the tree in the exact spot I requested. As the years rolled on I would often look at the tree and think to myself that the tree used to be bigger."

Michael (case 74). NDE at age thirteen months, sudden crushing blow. "Something fell on me and I lost consciousness for about 45 seconds. Best recollection is that I was choking and crying when I regained consciousness. My father and another adult male did something to get me breathing again. Since I recovered with minimal assistance and quickly, little was made of this. My mother was greatly concerned. Bright light and primary light experience; aware of dark light but not sent there. Clear body memory recovered of crushing pressure on my chest. While sequentially in the bright and primary lights, received five messages which I cannot recall, but want to."

Kelly (case 97). NDE at age three, drowning. "My brother, who is still living, said I came out of the water with a big smile on my face, laugh-

Michael, NDE age thirteen months

ing and giggling. My family talked about it many times as they thought I drowned because I was out so long and there was no sight of me. I was washed ashore later. I remember leaving my body as I was getting pulled out. I went into the Light and Jesus and other divine beings were there. I asked why I was there and they told me that they knew my life was difficult, and I was having a hard time. They wanted me to remember my mission and to remember the Light. I remember feeling bathed in Light, Love, Peace, that I hadn't known while in this body. They intended that. It gave me strength to go on as there wasn't much I could do about my living circumstances. I returned into my body and magically washed ashore, not upset at all. I have had a 'healthy' fear of the ocean since then. I love it, but it takes some talking to myself to feel secure in the water."

Heidi (case 67). NDE at age five, had been in hospital <u>several</u> times, including one from a head injury and another other from an accidental aspirin overdose, when she had a powerful "vision." "In the vision is a Lady of Light. I remember thinking of the Lady of Light as a 'queen' of some kind, but I had never heard of anything involving the Catholic religion (or any religion that speaks of a Divine Mother). I woke up very happy and puzzled by it. A year or so afterward, I was molested by a man on the street. I was so young I had no words to explain it to my parents. The trauma went pretty much unresolved, yet I felt somehow protected, and off in my own introspective world. I felt like an old soul."

Heidi, NDE at age five

Aiwen (case 96). NDE at age four, drowning. "I felt so pulled by the water I decided to jump in. I did not know how to swim but thought somehow it was easy. This was not the case and I just simply sunk to the bottom, even my paddling with my hands did not help me surface. I just felt myself drifting to the bottom of the pool. At one point I was looking downward and saw a slight light coming through, and then suddenly I was surrounded by beams of soft golden and pink and white light. The light was so alive and peaceful. I felt so comforted. I noticed the light seemed to glide through my spirit. I felt like the water and light were a part of me, then I was out of my body. I did not see my body but felt it floating above me as if I was attached by a string. I looked at this light surrounding me and then I saw bubbles arise. They circled around me. From within them mirror-like screens appeared and I saw within these glimpses of the universe, the other side, the reason why we are here, and other sacred mysteries that seemed to open for me and give me their truths. I had a small life review that revealed I was a loving, devout, tender boy, with a great gift. I was shown many pieces of my life from birth to family unions and holidays, then I was back in the pool, and that is when I saw the light beings. They had human forms with rainbow color, soft golden energy around them. They were like angels. They had their arms stretched out to me. They were so beautiful. They made me feel that I was okay and taken care of, like all my senses were part of a higher self, and I was becoming that higher self. A voice called out to me: 'You are okay, you are taken care of, you are completely divinely loved, there is nothing to be afraid of. You are sent here but it is not your time. You will help others see the light. We are with you.' I saw my destiny as a small child then, and felt deep within me I would help others throughout my life. I saw that love, and our bonds with others are the keys to this reality, and how we can cross over. My mother saw me in the pool and grabbed me and pulled me out. This happened so fast but it felt like forever."

Alma (case 55). NDE at age one, dehydration; NDEs at two and a half, three, and four when raped repeatedly by man in home— grandmother finally saw this and forced him out. "It was during this time that I experienced my first visit to a place not of Earth, when my abuser would mount me, covering my nose with his stomach area. I would suffocate and pass out. I can vividly remember his face as he sat waiting in the corner chair of the room, first staring at me for what seemed like a long time, then getting up to walk over to me, no pants on, smelling of alcohol, then my little arms moving in the air and my little legs feeling cool. I recall three more NDEs. I see my abuser sitting and staring at me with a look of being possessed by something not good. I smell the alcohol as he approaches, and I feel the heaviness of his stomach. I am still. I do not cry. It is dark for a short period, then everything went dark. It is very calm where I am now, and the aromas are sweet like perfume, like hundreds of flowers. I am floating inside of a large White Light. I can see the Light is all around me. It feels like I

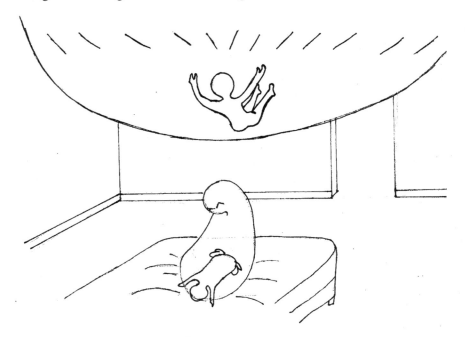

Alma, multiple NDEs starting at age one

am on a giant fluffy warm hand, like a comforter in the form of a hand, clasping me. It also feels like I am submerged in the White Light, as if it is a calm warm water all around me. I know I am safe and I am being loved. This is what I know the most: I am loved, very loved, very, very, very loved, and am safe, very, very, very safe. When the abuse stopped I was almost five. I was awakened by my abuser's hands one early morning. I began to tremble. I resisted by holding my head firmly from the pull of his hand and I moved my head from side to side. I remember his voice and then my voice. I said, "No." At that moment my grandmother, God bless her, walked into our home and saw through the bedroom door and yelled loudly for him to move away from me. That was the last time this relative ever touched me."

Deborah W. (case 48). NDE at age four, head trauma. "I awoke from having been slammed by a steel cart on wheels at a department store, pushed by an attendant not noticing the young child who stepped on the path of his pushcart. I was slammed so hard—the memory is with me today—I was thrown in the air and fell, face down, beneath the clothing rack where my mother stood. This experience was so compelling to me. I was awed and amazed at seeing my body on the ground, people gathering around, the interesting ornate ceiling of the big store, the place where my spirit-body hovered. Strangely, I seemed to be sitting, so gently swinging, on a light fixture way above the crowd. No fear about the height. I could see the whole department floor laid out in sections, watching people gather around a body on the floor. Saying this now, my heart is touched for the child and mother's experience—yet the hovering above, the I of me, felt no sense of attachment. I was simply an observer, without past or future. Then, a pulling energy like a huge rubber band snapped back, different than gravity—there was no sense of falling—a quality of elasticity pulled me, and I was drawn into the body on the floor. I remember the impact to my head—like a train— my body landing face down. I awoke on the ceiling, looking down on the scene, curious yet totally uninvolved with the people, aware of my new perspective, and content to be as I was forever more."

Audy (case 39). NDE at age three, abuse and attempted murder by babysitter. "I heard the clunk of the lock. The babysitter looked at me a few seconds, knelt a knee on the tub, grabbed my neck, covered my mouth, and shoved me under the water. When I tried to breathe I felt the water come through her fingers and it burned. I opened my eyes and all I could see were the bubbles above me. I could hear myself gargling, then all of a sudden I'm out of the water, and then back under again. She did this a few more times. The last time I remember my body feeling exhausted then everything went quiet. The next thing I knew I'm standing at the top of the tub looking down at my body. I see her pressing all her weight onto me, my legs are barely kicking. I'm confused because I know this is me but that was also my body, too. I could see my mom upstairs dressing my brother, someone was walking through the kitchen, and my dad was driving his old tan Ford home from work, and he's thinking about a lot of things. I looked at my body again, then turned around, and I see this long spinning tunnel with a really bright white light at the end. It was so bright, but it didn't blind me. I started moving down the tunnel and realized I'm floating. As I get farther I feel this huge wave of Love come over me and completely embrace me. Every cell in my being is overwhelmed by feelings of Love. Like every person's love on this earth I felt a million times over. All the pain disappeared. Nothing else mattered by what I felt in that moment. As I move, I see off to the right side big green fields and flowers in them. Now I am in the field looking at a patch of orange flowers and I'm holding one. When I look into it I see more than a thousand colors, some colors I've never seen before, all of them radiating this Love. Every blade of grass was so bright and alive! When I looked into this flower I felt like I was looking at a piece of myself. I was whole—One with everything surrounding me. I then heard 'go back' in a soft voice. I didn't pay atten-

Audy, NDE at age three

tion to it. Again, it says even louder, 'go back, go back!' When I held still to hear more, I felt this weird sucking speed, then I was in complete darkness. It felt like the womb, but all nurturing. The next moment I felt the speed again and, like a truck hit me, I slammed into my body. I came all the way out of the water as if standing on my feet. The most excruciating pain ripped through my entire body and my head felt like it was exploding. My chest was heavy. I cannot explain how much pain I felt. Simultaneously as this was happening, I heard a knock on the door. She removed me from the tub, wrapped me in a towel, and when she opened the door there was no one there."

Kelly (case 84). NDE at age two, drowning. "It was drawing me to it, the crystal blue water, so still. As my mother and grandmother were distracted, I slipped off my towel and jumped in. I could feel myself sinking to the bottom and could see a tunnel of light. I felt a huge gasp of pain in my chest as I swallowed the water but I was overwhelmed with a sense of light and love around me. I could hear my mother scream and watched her jump in. She said I was not under for longer than a minute, but I left my body and was limp when she pulled me out. I could hear her calling my name, but the sound became faint and I moved towards the lighted tunnel. It was a clear tube. I was weightless, out of my body, rising above the pool. It felt like I was gone for hours or days. I followed the light, where I saw a small horse come my way. He was yellow in color with giraffe-like spots. His tail was like that of a Raggedy Ann doll and orange yarn-like. He spoke with a soft voice and called me towards him. I was not afraid. He smelled of flowers and a scent I could not recognize. I walked with him, knowing I was not in my body, yet I did not feel spirit-like. The tunnel around me turned into a room, one of infinite borders, and filled with the most incredible sense of love. The horse introduced himself as Cody. He said he would be with me throughout my life, and when I reached 'double-twos' I would recognize who he was. He said I had the spirit of a 'Mary' and was sent here to fight and become a fighter for all. His words imprinted my soul. I remember wanting to stay. My biological father was hurting me, and I did not want to be in that body. He told me I would be back a few times and could call him when needed. He told me that God loved me and that I never needed to be afraid of anything. Just like that, he

Kelly, NDE at age two

kissed my forehead and the back of my neck, then the room dissipated. I felt my chest heavy and my body on cold tiles, my mother screaming and hitting my back. I threw up a lot of water and took a huge breath. I was back in my body and back on earth."

Joyce (case 110). NDE at age five, head split open by axe. "We lived in a tar-paper shack in California that had huge piles of mill-end blocks of wood. My older sister and I liked to sit on them and draw pictures. One day I was doing just that, and my older sister was splitting blocks with a double-bit axe. When she raised it over her head, it was too heavy and the axe fell behind her where I was sitting. It came down and split my head open. They thought I was dead, then I recovered and started to do strange things. For most of my life afterward I told myself I must have dreamed what happened to me when my head split open—except for one basic fact—the being I saw then. I knew nothing about Jesus but I instantly recognized Him. There was no tunnel, no bright light (golden instead), and no dead relatives. Yet I did things afterward, like riding a horse bareback, even jumped a creek. I just knew how to do this. I started singing songs from the 'forties.' Nobody could believe any of this. I was different."

Uwe (case 106). NDE at age two, suffocated. "I have no conscious memory of suffocating. Years later my parents informed me that I had nearly died when almost two. I was somewhat shocked and asked for details. We were living in the Russian Zone near the Elbe River of Occupied Germany at the close of World War II. My parents were desperately trying to escape the oppressive regime of the Russian/Allied victors. We were living in a very tiny village and were visiting a relative. I had been put to bed while the adults socialized. At some point, my Mother told me she went into the bedroom for something and noticed that the sizeable and very heavy headboard pillow had fallen on top of my head. She pushed it up and noticed I was not breathing properly.

Uwe, NDE at age two

She told me that if she came in a bit later, I would probably have suffocated. One memory surfaced only a few years ago: when about six or so I played that I had been crucified—like I knew about that."

*

I wanted you to know about Uwe. Although he has no memory of what happened to him, he grew up exhibiting the typical aftereffects of a child who had had a near-death experience. Children are like this. Because of home and school pressures, they can tuck away memories that don't seem to fit the life they are called upon to live. It's their behavior that gives them away. They just don't "fit in" like other kids no matter how hard they try, even within their own family. They wind up growing up decidedly different, without ever knowing why.

There's a judgment factor here, and it's a big one. So, let's face it now. If a doctor does not pronounce you clinically, fully dead, virtually a corpse, then whatever "tale" you tell about the life you experienced on the other side of death—what you saw, who you spoke to, anything you learned—is labeled "your imagination" or "a hallucination." Claims about near-death-*like* experiences, where people who are not actually close to death or even physically compromised can undergo patterns of experience and aftereffects virtually the same as near-deathers . . . well . . . they're not believed, either.

Hear this: today's medical and investigative research has established that *the phenomenon is real.* Yes, some lie about what happened to them, stretch the truth, or try to mold their experience to fit preferred beliefs. Yet the overall patterning holds true, irrespective of individual, religious or political interpretations, or country.

Birth and womb memories have both passed initial clinical testing, yet the general public still winces at any truth to such claims. Why? Because if we can prove truth to such realities, all of us, everywhere, must then *redefine consciousness and the inner workings of life itself.*

FOUR

Birth Memories

*I did not want to be born. Doctor pulled me out with a
pair of pliers.*

LUC (CASE 98)

*J*ohn Liona had a near-death experience inside his mother's vagina
as he was being born: the cord strangled him. His story and the
drawing he did to depict what he saw is in that first book I wrote about
child experiencers.

People like John call themselves "birthers," a name that identifies
those who remember being born, dying, and then coming back to life.

Don't laugh. Most birther memories are surprisingly lucid and clear.

Not just birthers talk about this. So does Dr. Raymond Moody
after he interviewed a man with total recall of a near-death experience that happened while he was in an incubator, weighing but three
pounds. Cherie Sutherland also wrote about such cases, like that of a
woman who, as a preemie, remembered a "big star thing in a great light"
with people trailing bubbles of colored air.[1] Some of the best evidence
of birth memory, though, comes from the clinical hypnosis of mother/
child pairs to cross-check memories,[2] and from the incredible work
of Dr. David Chamberlain with those who remember their birth and
being in the womb.[3]

To clear up any doubts about memory, let's admit right off that thanks to medical science we know that the human brain has an almost unlimited capacity for memory. Anything repetitive or rhythmic is more easily remembered, that's why we love music. Should emotions wrap around a memory, well, nuggets like that are hard to forget. Emotional memory can even rewire body responses—for a lifetime. All parts of our bodies have memory, not just the brain. It is true of creation itself. *Memory is core in the lifestream.* (Some refer to it as the "luminous lifestream.")

Knowing this, consider that of all the 120 people in this study, *93 had vivid memories of what happened to them—either as a babe or child or "tadpole"—irrespective of their present age.* And, in each case where I could contact relatives to double-check whatever they could recall, stories matched.

Be amazed at what follows.

Marianthi (case 53). "I had a premature birth because of an emotional shock my mother received. She was on her 7th month of pregnancy and heard that the Guerilla Resistance Army was coming down the mountains. I witnessed from a high angle in the hospital room, when the nurse who held me told the doctor, 'Come on, normal-born babies these days die, so you think THIS one is going to live?' I followed her from high up near the ceiling, where my awareness seemed to be, as she carried off my tightly swaddled little body. The nurse (who had her hair pulled back in a peculiar bun) took me to a dark room with a few cots and left me there. Two of the cots had similar bundles but they did not move. I would feel my tight little body full of pain and great dryness, so I would come out of it and hover near the ceiling where I felt fine. Every time I would go back into my body, the discomfort would drive me back out. I eventually decided to stay out, near the ceiling. Then a glow appeared to my right, slightly above me. I felt it was an intelligent companion who was there for my benefit. It conveyed a thought to me (telepathic): 'Do you want her to die? Go back to her (meaning the bundle that was me) as much as you can stand it, and I will make sure you will be alright.' The glow felt like a very wise male presence. I did what was suggested, then I found myself hovering over another place in the hospital where my grandmother had just arrived. She exchanged agitated words with the staff, boiled herbs in the hospital kitchen. She held the bundle that was me and spooned repeatedly what was in the pot into my mouth. I did not hover any more but stayed in my body."

Nathan (case 19). "My pre-birth memory is that of viewing my mother holding my older brother trying to settle him for sleep, walking down a hallway. I come through a wall or a door above and behind my mother's right shoulder, and I merge into her body where a baby would be."

Carol (case 45). "I had a cyst removed from my breast the day I was born. I remember waking up, being conscious and watching beautiful rays of sunlight streaming through a window, into my cradle, which

I'VE HAVE ALWAYS HAD THIS MEMORY MY MOTHER WALKING DOWN HALLWAY HOLDING MY OLDER BROTHER — ME DRAWN AS A SPHERICAL ENERGY MOVING AND MERGING INTO MOTHER'S BODY WHERE A BABY WOULD BE

Nathan, prebirth memory

was surrounded in pale pink bedding. I tried to discern 'things' float-ing in the rays of light. I remember understanding they were some sort of loving beings and communicating with them. I felt loved. I felt safe. I remember 'music' coming from the light. My heart overflowed with love, joy, fascination. I knew I was not alone. I was part of and con-nected to all that was going on. I knew in that moment that I was a part of God."

Catherine (case 73). "Breech birth, feet presentation. I remember coldness of air on my left foot and hanging around in darkness, not sure where I was. Not frightened in the aloneness, just very confused. Darkness was soft. I listened to the nurses. I seemed to be hearing them, understanding them. Might be shift change. One explains to others what happened to me. I hear 'poor little tyke, mother does not know.' They are speaking of my limpness, nonresponsiveness. One nurse brings the other over to look at me. I get a message: 'Be animated, move around.' I 'smile' and start to kick my arms and legs. One nurse says to the other: 'What are they talking about, she is fine. Look at her.' The other nurse comes rushing over, somehow I could see this. Second nurse remarks: 'Well, she wasn't like that an hour ago.' Back in crib looking up at them, am delighted that somehow I had happily surprised them. My mother said they would not let her see me for three days. Nurses said they did not have clean baby bedding to present me. Mom told them she didn't care. My father had brought in baby blankets. They wouldn't let him hold me as I was sleeping. My mom said none of this made sense, but she and dad were just kids and didn't know hospital protocol. There was no public health care in Canada at that time; no insurance."

A. H. (case 65). "I was born in the front seat of a brand-new Lincoln on a dark and rainy morning in the winding hills of western Pennsylvania, to a father who was a medical doctor and a mother who was suicidal

A. H., born to protect mother

during the pregnancy. I was born to prevent my father from killing my mother. I fought for my life. I saw what was going on. I had an adult voice and understanding by age three."

Sabine (case 100). "This is not a hospital situation. I am born at home. There was a nurse by my mother, who cut her open. I had a birth-nearly-dead experience. I saw that I was born happy. I saw the good things that would be in my life, and the painful traumas."

Marian (case 12). "I was desperately homesick and terrified at where I found myself after I was born. I had memories of being 'home' and of wanting to go back there. It was a world in the clouds, a world free of fear, just loving and joyful. I always felt 'other' here. I began having out-of-body experiences very young."

Sandra, born with a caul

Sandra (case 28). "I was covered in a white film, a caul, at birth. I have a vision/intense feeling in my mind, begging God to let me come to earth. I can picture myself, not God. He just is! I begged and begged him to let me come. I said: 'I know I can show them how to love you. I will love them, and they will know you. They need me.' Now, here I am and it has actually been easy to keep my promise to love even against many trials and failures to 'save' people."

Vicky (case 24). "I remember being able to leave my body, fly around the room, and being pulled back into my body. What prompted these OBEs was my dad having me propped up on the couch as he sat next to me. He'd lean in close with his big smiling face and tickle me under my chin. It made me laugh so hard I would fly up through the top of my head and out of my body. From the ceiling I'd look back at my little body on the couch and my dad sitting there laughing with me. I could see my mom in the kitchen ironing something on the ironing board. I could see the whole house while soaring around, and then suddenly swoop down back into my body. While I was out I wanted to stay out, but something always pulled me back. It was as if there were two parts of me. One aspect was me as the baby. And the other aspect was me with an adult mind. While I was out of my body I was me—but older, wiser, much more knowledgeable. When I returned to my baby body, it was as if I forgot that other aspect of myself. As I continued to go out, I remember telling myself that I must remember this."

Chester (case 54). "At my birth I remember being in some kind of bright light shining far away. I felt very peaceful, comfortable, and happy. All of a sudden, I thought that I must have reached the light because everything around me became bright very quickly, and it was very noisy. I felt like I woke up from a nice long sleep. I had a strange feeling of 'now I exist'—something very different had happened to me.

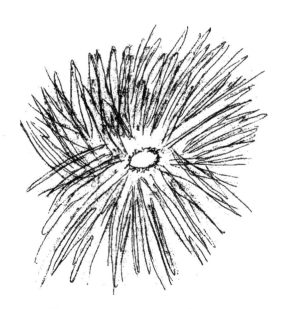

Chester, birth memory of chaos

I became aware of myself. Many feelings rushed into me. I was overwhelmed with the feeling of life. There were lots of people and they were chattering. This place was very different from where I had been. It was confusing, loud, and chaotic. I felt fearful. I wanted to go back where I came from. I was born with obstructed intestines and had to have corrective surgery same day."

*

In almost one voice, those who remember being born have this to say to doctors, nurses, and hospitals:

- Soften the lights in the room.
- Turn down the sound, maybe play soft music.
- Warm up the place, as well as the sheets and blankets.
- Medical instruments scare babies; explain their use as if babies understand.
- Watch what you say; babies listen—even if they are crying.
- Watch what you think; babies hear thoughts too.
- Assume babies have intelligence and memory.
- Out-of-body experiences are the main way babies explore.
- Tiny ones do not understand jokes.
- Loving touch is as important as milk, maybe more so.
- Rocking chairs are essential; gentle hugs too.
- Speak in conversational tone, forget "baby talk."
- Newborns respond to the invisible, as well as to you.

Parents, pay attention. These suggestions are not just for doctors, nurses, and hospital staff. Newborns are still connected to multiple worlds, so give them a little time to figure out the terrain changes. Trust love.

Birth memories illustrate that babes have an identity of their own, above and beyond anything they may have inherited. It is not at all unusual for two- or three-year-olds, even older, to suddenly rattle off "eyewitness" accounts of their own birth—much to the shock and amazement of parents.

Leonard D. Orr discovered a way through breathwork to enable adults to go back and reexperience their own birth. This method, called Rebirthing Breathwork, has proved effective. Practitioners of the technique can now be found worldwide.*

---

*Leonard D. Orr is the discoverer of the "rebirthing" technique, a way to remember and reclaim memories of birth/being born. He also founded the worldwide Rebirthing Breathwork movement. To learn more about him and the rebirthing technique, access his Rebirthing Breathwork International website or write to him at Rebirth International, PO Box 1026, Staunton, VA 24402.

FIVE

The Womb

It was like I was an adult in there.

HOUSTON (CASE 89)

omb memories are impossible. Docs claim this because myelin sheathing (the membrane that insulates nerve fibers) is not complete at birth. Or even before birth. Guess what? *Nerve fiber insulation actually begins a few weeks after conception and continues until adolescence.* Medical research now shows that preborns do a lot of thinking, and they're great dreamers.

Oh, by the way, *preborn* is now the proper term, not *fetus*. This change does not reflect anyone's religious belief. Nope. It reflects instead the continuous march of science and what medical investigators keep finding.

Here's a quick review of some of those "womb findings":

- At three weeks, embryo has head/tail, early spinal cord, swims
- At four weeks, heart and digestive tract are intact, blood circulation
- At five weeks, arms/legs bud out, heart pumping
- At six weeks, brain, eyes, ears, liver develop
- At ten weeks, all basic structures are in place, functioning; genital areas respond to stroking, body/brain integration

- At two months, react to strokes of fine hair around cheeks, bend body and extend arms/shoulders to push hair away; sensitive to touch, face reacts (is expressive), and does regular exercises with rest stops
- At twelve weeks, can suck on fingers, hands, toes; drinks amniotic fluid, develops a "sweet tooth," alcohol and nicotine from mother can throw off systems; detects differences in sounds/speech
- Around the same time, full thumb-sucking begins; respiratory system engages, liquid breathing (tiny sacs store air in lungs— this does not end until child is eight years old; thought to be why fresh air, playing outside, is so important for youngsters)
- At five months, males have a scrotum/penis, by twenty-six weeks can have an erection while sucking thumb/touching their thighs; perhaps sexual feelings
- At five months, "cry prints" of preborns have the same quality for identification as fingerprints once born; clear evidence for learning and memory, especially of speech/accents/sounds, vocal muscles develop (the womb is a sound chamber)
- At six months, can roll around like a well-rehearsed gymnastic specialist

One more goody: preborns determine the duration of pregnancy, which way they will lie, and how they will present in their mother's labor. Each has definite tastes and preferences and knows their mother's face *at birth*.[1]

Okay now, here's where we switch points of view from womb features to womb inhabitants.

Janee (case 113). "In the womb, my point of view started at the roof level of a car within the car; from space between front and back seats. Inside car looking down: Dad's door opens, he's hanging out of the car. Mom's just slumped with head down. No blood. No gore. Beautiful blue-sky winter day (timing probably within first trimester). Car had hit side of concrete bridge rail, bridge over small sparkling river with ice on sides, water flowing swiftly. Then I was outside 'floating' over the river near the bridge."

Penny (case 33). "Sometime after my fingers and toes were separate, though I recall them being webbed and liking that they were now separate, I liked how they felt in my mouth. The most profound memory was my mother smoking. I recall her anxiety, and I remember tasting the strange cigarette smoke taste. I remember getting excited in utero when she would feel anxious—because I knew that the bad taste was coming and soon I would feel high."

Dorothy (case 83). "I was an ectopic pregnancy, lodged in the fallopian tube. No one suspected pregnancy since my parents were both such devout Catholics. They finally agreed on an experimental procedure of

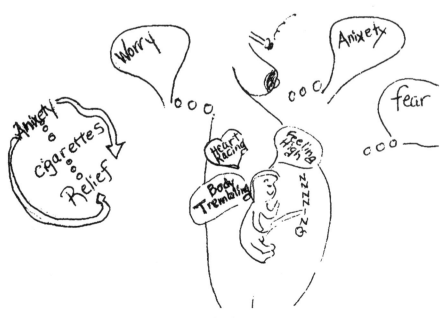

Penny, prebirth memory

forcing air into the tube—either I would drop down into utero, or not. In which case I would have either rotted where I was or kept growing until I burst both of us. There was a lot of shame and guilt with my mother. I was delivered via C-section at appropriate time. My inner journey there was being in Liminal Space, being so eager to incarnate on planet Earth at this time that I simply zeroed in on what I saw as the first available option. Only to 'wake up' horrified in the scenario of my parents' timeline—and declaring vehemently that I want to change my mind!!! I'm sure I can make a better choice. I was in a hurry."

Star (case 22). "What I remember pre-utero was a room with black living walls. There was an oval table in the center of the 'room' with a pedestal (just floating). I used black paper to draw on because all the background in the room was velvet black (floors, ceiling, and especially the walls—and they were 'breathing'), the crystalline table, the chairs. The skin tone of the Beings and the garments they were wearing were all a brilliant white. The fabric of the clothing was also 'breathing.' The small ball of light in the lower left-hand corner was me, where I seemed to be. There were seven sconces distributed on the 'walls' around the room. There was a crystal skull placed on each one. I was being instructed and 'set up' for my birth. The Being on my left began 'communicating' with me about my life path and the choices I was to make for this life. There were no words exchanged, only thoughts. We were near the end and I was preparing for my final 'choice.' It was the experience of Abandonment. A vortex appeared to my left. As it appeared, I noticed I was more of a brilliant light, more than 'a body.' I also noticed the vortex was pulsing in and out of the room. I was invited to move closer to the vortex and, as I did, the light that I was began to grow and glow more vividly. It was suggested that I look into and down the vortex toward Earth. As I did, I could see 'the heavens' and far off into the distance, Earth. Beautiful. Blue. Earth. I WAS PUSHED, and initiated into the Life of Abandonment! I had the feeling of being sooooooooo

Star, pre-utero memory

betrayed, so threatened, so lied to! I fell and fell and fell, reaching out with what I now saw as arms toward where I had been pushed. I have always had the feeling that as I was being born, I positioned myself with my feet braced against my mother's pelvis bone, yet gripping her pubic bone very tightly with my hands. I DID NOT WANT TO BE BORN. I felt so alone and terrified. My mother had two babies before me. Both of them died very shortly after their birth. I was born a year later. Every time my mother talked about these babies, I ALWAYS felt she was talking about me. I believe I was both of those babies. My mother wouldn't let anyone touch me because she was afraid I was going to get sick and die, too."

Marilyn R. (case 68). "As I am peering downward to planet Earth, God asks me, *Do you really want to go down and help those people that are unhappy and suffering?* 'I noticed the people needing help and I want to help them,' I reply naively. 'I want to go there to help them overcome

Marilyn R., prebirth memory

their troubles and sickness.' I remember staring down on the Earth and feeling great pain and misery. I know the people need help. I cannot handle their overwhelming despair that I feel and their illnesses. It saddens me to see such hurting. *You cannot help them unless you also experience what they experience,* God replies. 'I know how to help. I won't need to walk through those trials,' I retort. *You will be on a different level of communication without going through similar problems. The connection comes from having walked the same walk. When you walk through similar difficulties, you can then talk on their level of experience. People will listen when they can relate to your experience and your healing is evident. They will have hope because you have been there.*"

Monica, prebirth memory

Monica (case 103). "I have a clear memory of sitting on God's lap surrounded by angels. It really just looked like a big black filled with rainbowey light and an intense presence of love, but it felt like I was sitting on God's lap. He was looking at me and loving me intensely, and I looked at Him and loved Him back. I have always felt that love no matter what else has happened in my life. I am a daddy's girl. My angel was with me and I believe the rainbowey light was actually angels flying all about. I was sent back in the arms of my angel, to my mother, to prevent her falling into despair due to too much loss. I sought unceasingly to understand this strange place. I never felt like I fit in. It was as if I had dropped in from another planet."

*

Jaap van der Wal, Ph.D., a medical doctor now retired from the Department of Anatomy and Embryology at Maastricht University, Netherlands, travels the world teaching classes in what he calls the Embryo in Motion project. He is convinced that we are a consciousness having a body, and that an embryo is really an extension of the soul. To him, "the womb" is where the soul readies the body it will soon have to accomplish what lies ahead.[2]

Marianthi (case 53) says, "I saw that there was an intense glow that enveloped my parents at the moment of my conception." And Dr. Chamberlain admits that "it is disconcerting, but babies know more at birth than they could possibly have learned in nine months inside the womb. When and where could they have learned so much? Their mental activity seems to extend beyond the usual boundaries of time."[3]

A woman by the name of Ashley Stearns may have the answer. Ashley has what is called "hyperthymesia"—a condition of extremely detailed autobiographical memory, whereby she can remember a vast number of life experiences. "I had my NDE while being born. I can remember my birth, before my birth, my last in-between life, bits of other lives (an unresolved death I resolved when I was about three). I had access to 'the quantum fields' when I was young, most strikingly in a moment of crisis when I was five. Had great words to describe my timeless/spaceless experience ('omnipresent' and 'omnipotent') because of what happened consequently, but STILL couldn't talk about any of this to my Calvinist Lutheran family."

The reality of other worlds, other lives, other ways of being interweaves birth and death and whatever we think soul is. Clear-cut dividers don't exist.

SIX

Otherworldly

*My mother used to catch me trying to get to "the other side"
through the mirror.*

NICOLE (CASE 25)

$\int$pherical vision is commonplace for both child and adult near-
death experiencers during their episodes—and sometimes continuing for periods afterward. That's 360 degrees, all around, up and
down, in and out, backward and forward. For those born blind or who
become blind later, same deal.[1]

Missing twins and aborted babies sometimes appear and can speak
up, giving new meaning to the idea of "choice" and who's doing the
choosing. Unknown relatives pop in, too, during episodes, even secret
moms and dads. Animals are everywhere—sometimes as greeters on
the other side and sometimes as knowing guides. Little ones, especially,
see a lot of birds, small animals, and pets who have previously died but
returned as guides or helpers (true somewhat for adults except they tend
to see larger animals as well as deceased pets). *Don't ever think heaven
is just for people.* Angels? You name the color and size, winged or not—
there's plenty of them. Rarely, an alien.

Yes, there's a common pattern to near-death experiences worldwide.
But that common pattern tends to vary more with babies, infants,

toddlers, and small ones. It varies in *how it reveals the indescribable and the unimaginable.* Either in the womb, at birth, or afterward, many are shown, told, instructed, or come to know why they are being born, what their mission is, and the reason for any suffering or difficulty they may undergo.

In the article "Paranormal Aspects of Pre-Existence Memories in Young Children," Titus Rivas et al. write about the paranormal aspects of preexistence discovered in the prebirth memories of people like Vincent B.

> Just before he was born, he received a kind of preview about the life he would be leading. This preview came at a moment in time before his physical birth at which point he was no longer able to make any choices because he'd already chosen the parents he was going to be born to. He received what seemed like a guided tour and was shown incomplete, fragmentary images of his parents, himself, and the way he was going to be in the life to come.[2]

Interestingly, children seem prone to having multiple episodes while still young, with one or more as adults. It's almost as if one experience is just not enough. Teens differ in that any pattern to multiple experiences is not that clearly evident.

Here's a typical comment from a confused mother that will give you an idea of what I mean by "otherworldly": "My son who is now four years old had two near-death experiences while hospitalized. The doctor mismanaged his vent settings and blew holes throughout my son's lungs. He was given a 1% chance of survival. When he turned two, he woke up crying. He was crying about when he was dying. He kept saying that he did not think the Lady liked him anymore because he could not find her. He always describes his experience the same way, every single time. He says the Lady held him and God poured water on his head. He said they were both so beautiful. He said he only came back because God showed him that I was crying."

Understand that the very young are seldom given any reason why they must leave the other world or why the beings there abruptly disappear. Commonplace are stories of little ones doing everything they can to find "the bright ones" after they leave, convinced that it's their fault such loving beings are now gone. This is not silly nonsense. To the child this is serious business and can result in real guilt. Where has the Lady gone? What happened to the nice man? Doesn't God love me anymore? (Tiny ones do not use the word *angel,* rather, they use names like "bright ones" or "lights" or "stars." It is not until they are older, once they have heard the term *angel,* that they'll use it. And, yes, little ones tend to see angels with wings, perhaps explaining why the birds or butterflies they encounter "in death" are associated with the angelic, too.

The preborn and those newly born are often very concerned about the health and condition of their mother.

Neil A. (case 59) shares this. "At five weeks I was diagnosed with Pyloric Stenosis. This condition causes severe projectile non-bilious vomiting and is caused by a narrowing of the small valve in the stomach. It most often occurs in the first few months of life. No one thought I would survive. The memory of this event did not occur until I was twelve. I am convinced it was suppressed until then. It came to me as memory, not a dream. I remember seeing my parents in a very distressed situation, surrounded by people. A nurse told my mother there was still hope, that miracles can happen. Despite this assurance, my mother sobbed uncontrollably, which I found very uncomfortable. The next thing I knew I was in clear open space too beautiful for words. I remember the most wonderful vibrant, sharp colors, a million times brighter than anything I have ever seen. Bright lights everywhere, so bright it was inexplicable, but not so bright that my eyes hurt. The most wonderful music and the singing of words too beautiful to be spoken, extremely loud, but not painful—amazingly soothing. I was in the company of other beings, who somehow knew me and assured me everything would be alright.

I felt in complete peace, enveloped with love. I began to see the most wonderful strips of colors, like lasers, and they were touching my body and then radiating out into the ether. As they touched me, the feeling of peace and security increased beyond imagination. I began to communicate with other beings—no words—but we were speaking. Not in English but a language I somehow understood. 'You have many people thinking of you right now, and it is their prayers that you see.' A girl and a boy were with me. I felt a kindred association with them. I wanted to stay with them forever, but they told me, 'You have to leave for us.' Another being, a boy, clung to me tightly the whole time. He said, 'You have to go back to save Mother from the fire.' I didn't tell anyone about the experience until I was in my early twenties. My sister-in-law was five months pregnant when she miscarried. I took it very badly and went through stages of grief. My Mother told me not to worry as she too had a miscarriage before I was born. I asked her what it was like for her to have a miscarriage. She said, 'It was a living hell.' I asked her what it would have been like for her had I not survived. She said, 'I can't imagine how I would have coped. It would have been another living hell to deal with.' I thought of my near-death experience and of the boy who said, 'You have to go back to save your Mother from the fire.' Hell/fire. I understand now why I came back."

Gayatri (case 88) considers herself a double walk-in soul exchange. She claims she "awakened" to herself many times: during the first trimester in the womb, again several months later, then again at five weeks after birth and at four and ten years of age. Her words: "I saw all of the spiritual medical teams working on this vessel to re-animate the life force with walk-in consciousness. Yet the 4-year-old and the 10-year-old that I came down to merge with as a Higher Self aspect, did not transition right away (as is the case with most soul exchanges). Technically some medical intuitives call this procedure an OverSoul Merge, because we are all multi-dimensional beings of interconnected light, and this kind of integrative composite being is a form of "Energetic Synthesis." I could witness the layers of vibration that were being loaded back into the human form . . . so that the vital energy centers could be re-started or re-booted with the help of specialized spirit technicians. To say, afterwards was a massive adjustment is an understatement, yet I do remember not wanting or desiring to be here on this planet due to the fact that the assignment was so difficult, and there really wasn't a whole lot of support. I may have been four on the human bio-level, yet my core was so ancient and on such a laser focused mission that I just never fit in anymore in this dimension. My whole childhood was pretty much gone. I met my real parents, the Great Mother/Father Source, so human relatives around me didn't feel very loving or connected or even safe."

If you don't understand what Gayatri said, just know, on every level of her being, she considers herself from another planet and claims to have the ability to advance from one soul placement within her to another one as she advances in consciousness and matures in knowledge. I've spent some time with Gayatri and find her to come across as perfectly sane and focused. She is dedicated to helping others, especially children, and actively does all she can within welfare systems and through counseling to ensure that each child who needs supervision gets it, that each family awash in poverty and despair finds a home, and that each person wasted by drugs gets help. Her record of helping others is remarkable.

Deborah A. (case 79) barely survived scarlet fever at age three. Her memory of this did not return until the following year when, while gazing at the sky, she was suddenly overcome. "I was absolutely desolate and called out in my mind for the sky people to please take me. I was crying and crying. I could not fathom why they had left me behind. What had I done wrong for them to have abandoned me and left me in this strange place, this cold world. My mother and father seemed odd to me. I had flying dreams all the time and could not distinguish between dreams and waking reality. They were the same thing to me. I was upstairs in the hall of our 100+ year-old home, which had an extremely steep and narrow staircase leading down one flight. My five-year-old brother came upstairs and was standing at the top of the staircase when my mother called him. His back was to me, and I saw my opportunity. I bolted forward and pushed him from behind, yelling 'FLY!' To my absolute horror, I watched him plummet down that steep staircase and land at the bottom, screaming. Why hadn't he flown? I had nightmares after that. As I grew older, I viewed the sky people who left me behind as extraterrestrials, and myself as star seed." Deborah A. believes she was left behind by the sky people so she could become a walk-in.

Zoh (case 86) had a near-death experience at age three when she drowned. This began a long series of what she calls "high strangeness" when she was first abducted by aliens, then had an angelic encounter and spirit visitation, followed by talking with the dead, seeing the future, walking between worlds, incidents of telepathy, and an interest in stars. She says, "At four or five, I awoke in terror of seeing a short reptilian being in a little space outfit of sorts outside my window. From that day forward until I was 12, I pinned my curtains closed and slept with a light on. I was always terrified of being kidnapped."

Lillian (case 56) died during emergency throat surgery when she was three or four. She was born in Hong Kong of Chinese descent. She saw Jesus in her experience: "He spoke and told me I was only here for a short time. I had to go back. I frowned, seeing He meant it. I cried. I started to stomp my feet, bang my hands, and had a terrific tantrum. Jesus just stood where He was, watched me with compassionate eyes, and waited till I completely spent myself. Tired and exhausted, I hung my head down, sniffling from crying and standing before Him. Jesus looked over me with great patience and warmth. He said, 'It's not your time. There is work to be done.' I said 'I don't understand. Why can't I stay here?'"

Shortly after arriving in the States and while still a child, Lillian told the kids in school she had met Jesus when she died. Because she was reprimanded by her teacher for saying this, and by the other school kids too, she never mentioned it again. Throughout her life she has seen orbs around her that she believes are aliens. Later on she had a hypnotic regression that helped her to understand what had happened to her.

"I did not walk until I was two, didn't talk much," said *Dial (case 18)*. She remembers being in the womb and coming into this lifetime with a memory of eating only raw foods. She has a birthmark on her right shoulder that matches her memory of being shot there during a previous life, and it still pains her from time to time. She's seen many spaceships. "One time, I went to bed knowing that someone would be coming for me. Sure enough, two beings came and took me to their planet. I looked around and realized the people created the light, so I guess this would have been in another solar system. I was taken on a tour of the place, then taken to a leader. While he was talking to me [she doesn't remember anything said],

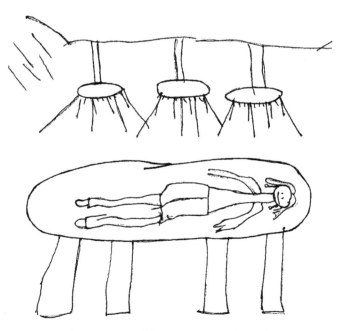

Dial, memory of being on another planet

I picked up a small sea shell. I asked myself, 'Can I take this home with me?' That was the last thing I remember. Next morning I woke up, not remembering a thing. I went to the kitchen. While walking to the patio, I stepped on the shell. It was on the floor. At that moment I remembered the night before!" She also remembers levitating and being with others on the other side and of numerous UFO encounters and being "examined" (refer to her drawing on page 53).

Twins are not necessarily who or what we think they are. Thanks to the latest in medical research, we now know about a "chimera"—the fusion of two bodies and two blood groups, perhaps even a third (in the case of triplets). This means that twins can exist without having any of their own mother's DNA. Around 8 percent of nonidentical twins and 21 percent of triplets have not one but two blood groups: one produced by their own cells and one produced by "alien" cells absorbed from their twin. Being then a product of two different cell lines, they likely could be carrying bits of their own sibling within their body and brain. These "parts" may even be influencing how they act—*even if they don't know they ever had a twin.** Strange but true, you can also be influenced during gestation by what remains in your mother's womb from a previous pregnancy.

This "science surprise" lays the groundwork for near-death experiences with or related to twins.

Caroline (case 42) was born "different." Thought to be autistic, it turned out that she had selective mutism (a complex anxiety disorder that restricts speech until the child feels comfortable and secure).

---

*The complicated reality of a chimera, of a mother unrelated to her own children, can be present with twins and triplets. It is possible for twins to merge into one body early in development. Being the product of two different cell lines, some of her eggs can carry a genome different from the rest of the body. There have also been court cases where it was found that there was no trace of a mother's DNA in her own children. See the article "Is Another Human Living Inside You?" on the BBC Future website.

She has an identical twin. "For as long as I can remember, my twin and I remembered a previous life. We would often talk about that life together, as we believe we were also sisters in that previous life. I recall we lived in a forest village somewhere that I can now identify as Europe. I see dark pine-tree forests surrounding a whitewashed stone cottage, or cottages, and we could even identify who lived in the other cottages, some of them by name. The surroundings are damp and musty, the colors are dark and muted. There is a lot of moss and dark wood (dead branches, etc.) lying amongst stones and rocks. I could even feel the coolness and perhaps even smell the dampness that comes with a forest. Since I was born in arid land on the central west coast of Western Australia, I had no way of knowing what a forest of that type would be like. My sister and I often talked about this."

Robyn (case 75) claims that her first recollection of conscious awareness in this lifetime occurred while still in utero. "Visual memory is of warmth, comfort, and being very alone in my space, but happy—yet somehow instinctively aware that I was not the first to have been there. It was like the one before me had left some kind of energy imprint, as if the stretch marks on my mother's stomach were in some way a form of cave painting—when the light of the outside world illuminated my space. There was none of the usual belly bonding while I was in utero. After my birth, it soon became apparent I was alone. The energy felt wrong. By the time I was five, I learned that an older sister, their first born, had passed away from pneumonia merely days after her birth."

Nathan (case 115) knows now why he has felt "double" all his life, that he was somehow not made for this world. Due to his mother's health, he had to be taken early, before his lungs were completely developed. As a result his lungs collapsed, and it was several weeks before he could be released from the hospital. During the first five years of his life, he was hospitalized repeatedly for pneumonia. He says, "I began to talk in full sentences from the age of three. I would tell my mother every night how an angel had come to take me away to heaven. By age twelve, I began to suspect that I may have had a twin. I had visited a psychic who told me that I did have a twin who had died at birth. I asked my mother about this. She verified that she had been in labor for 2½ weeks after I was born, though doctors told her it was just a hysterical reaction to her traumatic pregnancy. Later, because she couldn't walk, my father took her to the emergency room and they performed an emergency DNC [surgical procedure to remove contents of the uterus]. It was then that the doctor told her they had found my twin. When sixteen I had a dream where I felt an arm next to mine. I rolled over and up on one arm—I saw him—a boy who looked just like me. I asked who he was and how long he had been there. He replied that I knew who he was, that he had always been here. We talked late into the night and then had fallen asleep together. Sometime during the night, I had fallen off the bed on the side facing away from the door. Mom had come to wake me up and thought he was me and woke him up. I stayed down until she left and then I jumped up and we both laughed because she had mistaken him for me. Then the scene changed, and I was on the front porch waiting for him but awoke before he returned. Ten years later, my mother and father went to a casino in the mountains of West Virginia for a vacation. While there, she had a dream that a guy who looked identical to me was her waiter. She asked him when he was born and then she asked his name and he said Nathaniel. She told him she had his brother and went directly to a pay phone to call me, then woke up. My name is Nathan. His name is Nathaniel. I felt as if I was in his body and he was in mine."

Remembering past lives can become a real issue for kids who survive death, as their tender age denies the possibility of any such memory. Others' disbelief can confuse a child, especially in this culture where reincarnation is still considered fiction.

Paul, "holy picture"

Paul (case 6) was a breech baby. His head was wrapped tightly by the umbilical cord, with a membrane like a plastic bag covering his face, keeping him from breathing. During his earliest days of life he had visitations from small people who would come into his room at night, sometimes through an unopened window and sometimes through a cupboard from which they would pull all kinds of junk into his room— old clothes mainly and on one occasion a strange box that scared the daylights out of him. He says, "I was educated by nuns. When asked to draw a 'holy picture,' I drew a helmeted figure with a crest on top. The nun became quite angry and asked why I had not drawn a 'holy picture.' I explained that it was a soldier standing in front of a cave, and in my little mind I had done what she asked. Many years later as an adult I saw a Victorian print of Orpheus entering the underworld. It was what I had tried to draw. How would a child of five or six know about Greek mythology? My entire young life was filled with such events, including being expelled from Sunday School for challenging church authority over Jesus' ascent into Heaven, and even including diagrams of the internal parts of the Egyptian pyramids."

Nila's son (case 47) was born during an emergency caesarean because the cord was wrapped around his neck three times. Nila's mother Rhoda had died fourteen years before her son's birth, and her name was hardly mentioned. Yet when given a big teddy bear by his mother's friend, Nila's son named his new playmate "Rhoda." At around three years old, he began to report seeing deceased people and wondered why they were coming around him. He had many spirit visitors. On holiday he suddenly froze and began watching the room curtains intently. He whispered, "Look." When asked to describe what he saw, he described a young man with a scarf on his head who had died recently in a motorbike accident. Soon after, Nila describes, "he got a faraway look in his eyes as we were sitting at the meal table. He then said to me, 'You're nicer than my last mummy.' I asked him to describe her and he said she had long red hair and got angry easily. He described a fairly grand double-story stone house and his mother with a baby in her arms as she said goodbye to my son and his past-life father. They went away on business, but drowned on a boat that sank. He always pronounced certain words with a Scottish accent when he was little, and he always wanted to order me around as if I was a servant. This seemed quite natural to him."

Linda, a near-death experiencer herself, said her son *Daniel (case 95)* was deeply affected while still in her womb when she underwent an intense spiritual transformation. When he was two, he told her he had another father and mother, then became obsessively interested in the martial arts and exhibited a natural ability in it. She says, "Around four he fully identified with Chinese culture, food, using chop sticks, writing and speaking Chinese (even though it was made up), plus he would tell us his other family was from China. He said his father was a miner and his other mother worked in an aero plane factory. To everyone's amusement, Daniel, blonde with blue eyes, gravitated toward the Chinese. At the end of pre-primary, when he returned from school holiday, he told everyone he had been in China for the break. The truth is he had only been to local markets and had a Chinese lunch. We'd listen to him and accept what he was telling us. After a classroom news event, his teacher wanted Rob and I to discourage his China-talk. We disagreed with that approach. I told her plainly that I believed it was a past-life memory and he needed to work through it in his own way, his own time. She probably thought we were nuts, but that's okay. He did work through it and has become a determined and masterful young man with a good deal of social confidence and charisma."

Marcella (case 27) was born prematurely and had one health challenge after another until six months of age. She says, "During childhood I loved everything Medieval and British, much to the astonishment of my mother. I craved learning yet continued to favor England, especially during the Edwardian Era, 1850s to 1915. I observed myself dying in the water after the Titanic sinking. I seemed to be a man in his late forties, early fifties. That would make my birth then around 1870. I gravitate to nature-space-history documentaries, topics that are non-fiction. Fiction seems absurd to me. Another childhood experience I had was seeing a child's black and white drawing of an ocean tanker being tossed in a storm on the sea, at nighttime. I clearly remember, even to this day, the feeling of absolute terror which came up in me at seeing this picture. Even today I don't think I would like to open the same book to that page! Reminds me of Titanic."

Sandy (case 26) says she's had unusual memories since birth of another life before this one. "As a young child, I reminisced about my memories, yet was confused by them. I didn't understand how I had memories of doing things I had never done yet, like climbing trees with other children. I was too little at age three, yet I remembered having done so. I had only my mom to share this with, but she thought my memories were

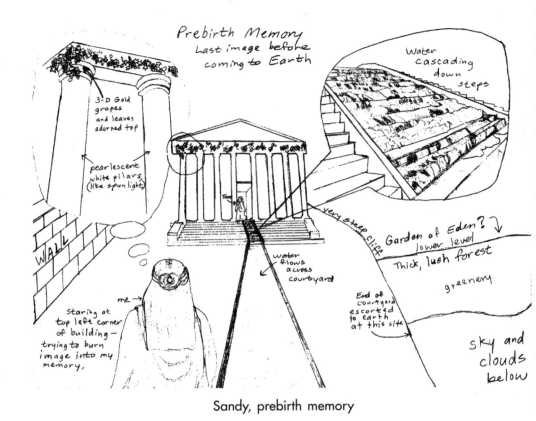

Sandy, prebirth memory

just dreams." This quandary continued well into adulthood until she discovered the writings of Socrates when he discussed this very thing with Cebes and Simmias. While writing a book about this,[3] Sandy met other people like her who were searching for answers—*people who recognized her from their own past-life memories.* They, too, related to Socrates, especially his discussion with Cebes and Simmias about life before birth: Cebes said, "It seems that we've managed to prove about half of what we wanted—that the soul existed before birth—but now we need also to prove that it will exist after death no less than before birth, if our proof is to be complete." Socrates replied, "It has been proved already."[4] Above is a rather elaborate drawing of what Sandy remembers of her life in ancient Greece.

Elaine, NDE as a newborn, memory of reality

Elaine's father, imprisoned in Iraq and then deported, had dysentery when he returned home to Scotland. *Elaine (case 34),* as a newborn, caught it from him, and nearly died. After that she was noticeably "odd" and said to have developed a nondominant brain activated by her illness. Her mother said she was in a "dwalm," a trance state. She developed a bad squint in her left eye, had no memory of her three siblings, and formed no friends when she went to school. She says, "People said I was weird because I wanted to be alone and was often silent, spending time in nature, feeling very merged with nature. I went to church with my grandmother, but no one else in the family went to church." Later on, she remembers a past life of death by drowning: "I was pulled from the water, taken to an island, laid on a flat surface, and covered with sheet. I knew I was not dead but I could not move or speak. I could see a woman, like a nun, with a candle moving round me, and I could see myself lying under the sheet." Elaine's memory of reality while growing up shows in this unusual drawing.

*

If you want to pursue the idea of reincarnation/past lives of kids, refer to the book, *Return to Life*[5] by Jim B. Tucker, M.D. Although he does not cover near-death realities per se, his work gives all of us solid, evidential research of children who remember lives that occurred at other times, in other places, long before their own birth "this time around." This book challenges everything you thought you knew about how life works.

This is a good place to bring up the subject of cryptomnesia. This refers to "hidden memory," where the subconscious mind records everything ever heard, read, or seen—whether in passing conversations, on television or radio, in books, newspapers, or movies, at conferences, etc. Our mind converts all of this to memory, the kind of memory that can become the foundation for what seems to be past-life or otherworldly realities. Processing is holistic. That means we tend to "fill in the blanks" to create stories that feel right.

Cryptomnesia falls apart in near-death studies when family members, medical people, or nearby observers are able to give third-party testimonials as to the accuracy of what happened (the event) and changes that occurred afterward (the aftereffects). This includes whatever seems otherworldly or spirit-led. Remember: for the very young, especially birthers, *there was no before.* What scientists mean by hidden memory takes on a whole new meaning with small ones. As they aged, though, could the experiencers I've quoted have stretched things a bit? Possibly. That's why I went after as many verifications, life stories, and aftereffects as I could find. What was claimed checked out with the vast majority of the 120 who participated this time and the 277 I worked with before.

What never ceases to amaze me is the wide-awake clarity of near-death experiences—especially with birthers, infants, toddlers, and the very young.

SEVEN

Some Surprises

God said to me, "Don't tell anyone. We will keep this between us."

NEIL H. (CASE 36)

*D*id you know that about 85 percent of children who experience cardiac arrest have a near-death experience? I found that numbers from drownings and parental/sibling/sexual abuse are even higher. This means that lots of kids go through a shift in reality *before* they know that much about what reality is. Who's more surprised when this happens—the child or the adult?

Adults talk a lot about "the light" they encountered on the other side. But kids are more specific about *what kind of light* they saw where they went. Here are the types they have described:

- *Primary light*—usually seen as a pulsating luminosity, a radiance that is almost frightening in how awesome and piercing it is, how powerful and all encompassing—as if it is "the origin of all origins"
- *Dark or black light*—sometimes described as black with purple tinges or just dark, a shimmering, peaceful, healing place some

kids call the Darkness That Knows—a source of strength and knowing, a sanctuary, like "the womb of creation"

- *Bright or white light*—can have a full range of yellow-gold-white hues, brilliant with an almost blinding glow that emanates unconditional love—a warm inviting intelligence, like "the activity of truth"

Rarely are black-light experiences negative. On the contrary, they are almost magical in the healing properties that particular light seems to contain, and how it enhances the faculty of knowing. Youngsters tend to label each type of these lights in this manner: bright light is the "Father Light," dark light is the "Mother Light," and that primary, powerful radiance is "God's Light." They are clear that Father Light and Mother Light come from God's Light.

An unexpected surprise emerged from this study: a fourth type of light called "Clear Light." What happened to *Uf (case 109)* is an example. Since she does not speak English, Christopher "Bob" Coppes from the Netherlands has acted as translator. (Thanks, Bob). I merely clarified what they said, so it could be better understood.

Uf was a "blue baby" (one with a heart malformation that prevents a baby's blood from being fully oxygenated), and not expected to live. She entered Clear Light when born, surprised everyone by surviving; then, at various times since, has re-entered that special light. Her frustration in describing any of this has revolved around the shame she felt as a child for "not fitting in" (whether with other kids or family), and when older for not being like other near-death experiencers. A study of Buddhism as an adult helped her to realize that Clear Light is the one said to unify all the energy centers of one's body— the glow of Joy/Vitality/Trust can result—the highest of healings through the greatest of lights. By focusing on the Clear Light of her death, she discovered how to help herself and others, how to heal.

Prayer beams—another surprise. While out of body, the young can often see light coming from anyone praying. They describe how the power of those prayers turn into beams of radiant golden or rainbow light. Seldom did any of them see horizontal stripes of color like what you see with rainbows. Mostly what they saw were vertical bands with brilliant white on either or both ends, as if the beams were long rods or rays. Kids showed me with gestures how that beam of light arced over from the one saying the prayer to where they themselves were hovering, no matter how many miles away. The majority of those who saw this light called it a "prayer beam." Once a prayer beam "hit" them, some said it felt like a splash of love. Others said it made them feel warm and tickly all over. Because they saw prayer as real energy that did real things and had a real affect, most of these youngsters went on to pray easily and often. Some even sent prayer beams back to God/Allah/Deity. What I've noticed with child experiencers once grown is that the majority of them continued to use prayer as a source of guidance and aid—irrespective of church or religion.

Lights, lights, and more lights. Children, once old enough to express themselves, point out a light they see coming from a woman's tummy if she is pregnant and from an individual's face or heart area if he is about to die. When I say "point" I mean just that—an innocent gesture that can be very embarrassing in public, or a heart-stopper at life's end. Kids are never wrong about this. Verification of what they see comes from science. That light at pregnancy? We now know that when a sperm meets an egg, an explosion of fireworks results. This light flash has been captured on film again and again. Always happens. Apparently, though, the glow of that light can continue for weeks, even a month or two.[1] That light at death? Well, scientists have seen a flash of light occurring whenever any organism dies, especially humans. The emission of radiation from this death flash is ten to one thousand times stronger than normal and contains information about the source that just released it.* These two very real lights conjure up all kinds of ideas and stories, especially of the spiritual.

Consider also here the Holy Shroud, stored at a church in Turin, Italy. It is believed to be the burial cloth to have covered Jesus after his crucifixion. It exhibits an exact imprint of the man's body it once wrapped, in both positive/negative formats and containing such detailed information that there is only one way this unusual imprint could have been made: with a flash photolysis, which is the breakdown of materials under an intense emission of radiation—a death flash.

Charmed and protected afterward? Dr. Penny Sartori in England noticed this quality.[2] Cherie Sutherland in Australia encountered the same thing.[3] What struck their attention is that near-death kids tend to lead "charmed lives" afterward, as if they possess some type of special protection, perhaps the "compensatory gift" of a heightened compassion and an extended range of intuitive perception that seems to aid them in understanding life's difficulties. Sutherland referred to the work of Dr. Kenneth Ring, one of the giants in near-death research, and his paper "Amazing Grace: The Near-Death Experience as a Compensatory Gift."[4] His paper strongly implies that changes in the lives of experiencers afterward show spiritual components that "change" them. Any "charm" these children gain afterward does not exempt them from heartbreak, but it does seem to make a positive difference in how they handle challenges.

That incredible charm and compassion many possess readily rolls over into lively conversations with and about critters and wee folk, as well as "the invisibles." By that I mean pets, birds, animals of all sorts—wild or tame—plus a whole range of "ghostly visitors" often labeled as "one's imagination."

---

*Research on this was originally done by Janusz Slawinski, a member of the faculty of the Agricultural University at Wojska Polskiego in Poznan, Poland. His work on the reality of a "death flash" was spurned at first, then upheld by other researchers. Refer to "Electromagnetic Radiation and the Afterlife," *Journal of Near-Death Studies* 6, no. 2 (Winter 1987): 79–94. Available on the New Dualism website.

Okay everyone; take a deep breath. We're taking a brief break here so you can finally know the *truth about imagination*. There are two aspects: (1) intentional fabrication, where we make it up from our own minds and feeling sense and (2) what is presented to us, intact, from a world that is as real as what we see, touch, hear, feel, and know intellectually. French scholar and mystic Henry Corbin,* coined the phrase *imaginal worlds* to describe realms that exist above and beyond the three-dimensional world, where things are *real* in the sense that they are not being imagined. Imaginal imagery has integrity and exists apart from what we create or control.

Let me reframe what I just said: Something imaginary is created by and comes *from* us. Something imaginal comes *to* us from another realm beyond our own making. When an imaginal image presents itself to us, we may be awed, afraid, surprised, puzzled, confused, or emotionally moved. It stirs something deep within us. It awakens us to a feeling or emotion. The imaginal realm carries within it "thoughts of the heart" that can awaken universal archetypes and deeper processes of creativity. *Archetypes,* as defined by renowned psychologist Carl Jung,† are "symbols with meaning" that can take on a life of their own and exist outside of individual consciousness, thus bridging the gap between objective reality and what is imagined.

Appreciating the difference between imaginary and imaginal helps you to understand child experiencers like **Monica** (case 103) who relates

---

*Henry Corbin was a philosopher, theologian, Iranologist, and professor of Islamic Studies in Paris, France. He was a champion of the transformative power of imagination and of the transcendent reality of the individual in a world threatened by totalitarianisms of all kinds. His great work, *Alone with the Alone: Creative Imagination in the Sufism of Ibn' Arabi,* is a classic initiatory text of visionary spirituality.

†Carl Jung was a Swiss psychiatrist and psychoanalyst who founded analytical psychology. His work has been influential not only in psychiatry but also in anthropology, archaeology, literature, philosophy, and religion. He was also a student of Eastern philosophy and had a near-death experience later in life that completely changed him and his message.

Monica, NDE at age one,
drawing of nature as a family

more to nature than people. She says, "I was on life support for two weeks as a one-year-old. The aftereffects have been with me all my life. I am sure this dynamic contributed to my inclination to want to rise to another plane. I sought unceasingly to understand this strange place. I never felt like I fit in. It was as if I had dropped in from another planet." Monica is quite an artist. This sketch of hers shows nature as family.

Reneé (case 80) was born premature and had a near-death experience a few years later at her babysitter's home. She says, "Little children who claim to have imaginary friends actually see real people. The portal between the pre-mortal world or spirit world and this realm on earth is not yet completely closed. Eventually this portal or veil is closed for most people. Although there are beings for whom this portal never completely closes, and they are blessed with special spiritual or paranormal gifts to bless the lives of others." Her memory of where she lived before being born is depicted in drawing below.

Before we go any further, the "alien" question needs to be addressed in terms of what I discovered in previous research, and what I know now.

Of the 277 experiencers in my earlier study, 9 percent claimed to be from another planet, 14 percent said they had been abducted by a UFO (spaceship), and 39 percent said they were from *another dimension*. Let me clarify that 39 percent. None of these kids related to being human or otherwise, having past lives, or belonging to any spiritual lineage or soul group. *None of them.* They identified instead with being part of the

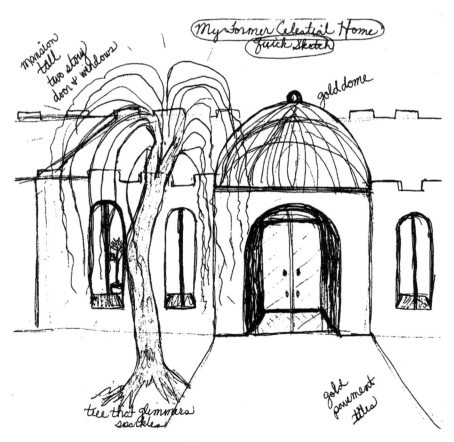

Reneé, NDE as a toddler, memory of prebirth dwelling

universe itself, maybe an asteroid or a standing wave or a crater on some planet or a gas vent. To them, saying they were from Venus simply meant they were once part of the planet itself. Their truth? Every bit and piece of the universe is *conscious;* each has volition, intelligence, and purpose.

These kids claimed that Earth had sent out an SOS call for help, that its environment, its very existence, was now in jeopardy. Their mission, the reason they came and were born into human bodies, was to help Earth itself. The "luminous lifestream" is what they claimed as home. Higher levels of spirituality and truth were more important to them than parents or family. Ecological sustainability—the "green" movement—was their goal. Specifics? They said they were here "for the changes." Time frame? When they had aged enough to have older children and/or retire. When I checked the age they were when I had sessions with them versus the age they indicated, I found that the time frame all of them warned about, when Earth would be under tremendous strain, was between 2020 and 2029.[5]

With the current bunch of 120? Two claimed to have been abducted by aliens and taken up into a space craft for a tour of other planets.[6] That's it. Yet 44 percent felt as if they must be from another world or another dimension because they certainly didn't fit this one. Allow me this: Feeling foreign, never fitting in, doesn't mean you're an off-worlder. It could mean that you're a typical experiencer of a near-death state either at birth or when you were an infant or a very young child. None of these children grow up feeling "normal."

Under the heading of "odd," several children spoke of being able to levitate after their episode, as if that was a perfectly normal thing for them to do. This ability tended to fade once the child was close to puberty. One of those reporting levitation is ***Janet (case 15).*** In the drawing below she shows herself levitating above her bed at the age of seven.

Again and again, throughout my forty years of near-death research, I have been baffled by the frequency of kids who said they could breathe

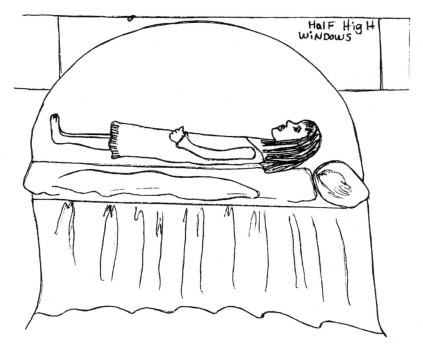

Janet, levitating above bed

underwater. That's why they never came up for air. Whether at the bottom of pools or lakes or streams—no problem—they just kept walking. Maybe they didn't feel a need for air, but their body sure did. Hence the near-death experience connected to so many drownings. I noticed this same trait with other kids, even my own son. He never panicked underwater when he was small. We did. We finally figured he must be "part fish." Still is, by the way.

I'm not trying to be cute here, but I think there's a connection between child experiencers who show little or no need for air while underwater and adult experiencers who do the same thing after their NDEs, during everyday life—no air coming in or out the nose, no lungs working, yet they're perfectly fine. Don't even miss the stuff.

I was one of them after my own three near-death experiences in 1977. On one occasion, I watched the car clock as I was driving in heavy traffic down Vista Boulevard to the capitol building in Boise, Idaho, then out to Floating Feather Airport off State Street (yes, I'm a native Idahoan now living in Virginia). I was alert and fully conscious the whole time. I began to wonder, though, that maybe my lungs ought to be involved in what I was doing. So, after about eight minutes or so, I pulled over to the side, parked my car, and engaged in prayer while visualizing the billows in my lungs working again and staying that way. This challenge I had with lungs and air continued for one year. Eventually, my lungs caught on and kept working.

This isn't a "me" thing. Untold numbers of near-death experiencers are like this. No, we haven't achieved some "holy reward" from dying and coming back, nor have children been "marked" as unique angels. It took my falling off a ladder in 2017 for that "nonbreathing," fully-operational-lung-and-brain-function state, to be duplicated. My vagus nerve took over. If you haven't heard of the vagus nerve before, know that it is the one that connects all our major organs and guarantees our survival during extreme conditions by pulling blood from our extremities and pooling it around our heart as it supplies needed oxygen to the brain. When I say the vagus takes over, I mean it. You cannot fight the vagus. That nerve runs things . . . you . . . and you breathe even when your lungs are offline, and your nose feels like it's on vacation.

From what I've seen and come to know from thousands of cases, including my own, it is now my belief that the vagus nerve is running the show when kids aren't breathing under water, and when many adult experiencers are able to continue on unabated sans lungs—as if nothing weird is going on.

Add this to your thinking cap: hardly ever does any near-death experiencer of any age see the fabled "silver cord"—what the various religions and spiritual traditions claim connects our soul with our body. No matter how torn up an experiencer's body is or how long without vital signs—again—rarely does anyone mention a thing about any type of connecting cord. Why? I'll bet it's because the silver cord never broke. The vagus nerve wouldn't let it. Why? Maybe because we still have work to do, here on planet Earth, wearing the body we have, living the life we were given. If I'm right about this, then that means the vagus nerve is the physical component to the silver cord.*

What else happens afterward? Turn the page.

---

*For many years, psychologist Karen E. Herrick, Ph.D., has been working on the puzzle of why most near-death experiencers say nothing about seeing a "silver cord" when they're out of body. In her work she discovered how powerful the vagus nerve is and how one can be trained to "breathe" through the vagus directly, and her findings have been important in my own research. She now teaches classes in vagus breathing. You can find her contact information in the "Resources" section.

EIGHT

Afterward

I told my younger brother about what I remembered, and he told my mom. She got angry and said, "He is not supposed to remember things like that!"

WARREN (CASE 51)

Random comments experiencers made:

Penelope (case 87). "Anytime I sensed that people were being motivated by selfishness and malice, it would upset me and make me cry. There were TV shows that I couldn't watch because I would become too upset."

Heidi (case 67). "I can see accidents before they happen. I even grieve at the death of a fly or a moth or a mouse."

Joshua (case 69). "My brain is like a sponge now. Always speak from my heart. Answers are within."

Marianthi (case 53). "Before I learned to speak, I understood adult conversation. I could willfully stay under water for long periods; was a champion swimmer."

Sherryjane (case 58). "As a toddler, I could name every make and model of cars on the road; was put in a school for the gifted."

David (case 61). "Memories of 'elsewhere' have haunted me throughout my life. I drew pictures of my birth over and over again."

Carol (case 45). "As a young child I could make lights go off and on. Objects moved just by my thinking it so."

Deborah W. (case 48). "Must be silent about 'my invisible life.' Developed two lives: one intellectual with my family, the other intuitive with angels. Parallel realities, parallel worlds. This helps me help others."

Marianne (case 111). "I spent a long time standing at the mirror in my room, just to see if I existed."

James (case 99). "As I got older I had trouble understanding the concept of worship. God? Who or what is God? I developed a concept of the devil. By age five, I imagined having a battle with the devil in the bathroom wherein I won the battle by flushing him down the toilet."

Jan (case 7). "I have felt different from most people. Over time, I have realized how different I am. I see, feel, and remember things most people don't."

Audy (case 39). "I get this fire in my stomach and my body vibrates intensely like adrenaline, and I feel so passionate it rings in every cell and I am surprised by the words that come out of my mouth. I didn't know I could have so much knowledge."

Damon (case 112). "Throughout my life I felt mature, well beyond being a child. I felt more like an adult in a child's body. I didn't feel bonded to my parents or brothers. I longed for something indescribable in the distance. I would feel desolate, wanting to be 'out there.' I didn't feel connected to other children either."

Janee (case 113). "Nothing was important but EVERYTHING was important. Soul pain. Felt like I was kicked out of heaven, and then a huge thick dense wall was built between my Real Home and God and me. I was so, so, so mad at God for a long time."

Surprising research percentages:

Virtually all of the 120 cases displayed strong intuitive abilities (inner knowing, inner sensing, inner awareness). Most were also psychic (in tune with movements in the outer worlds of people and events). A full 90 percent either lost or never formed any bonding with their parents (three-quarters of that number bonded instead to bright ones on the other side, like spirit or angelic beings).

Those who became empaths—84 percent. Developed deep, strong emotions—75 percent. Highly intelligent, many to the point of genius—75 percent. Suicide prone—74 percent. Vivid dreams, often predictive—70 percent. Can't sleep well or has sleep issues—67 percent. Difficult family situations—62 percent. Out-of-body experiences commonplace—62 percent. Sees the future, can also have future memory episodes (pre-live the future before it occurs)—61 percent.

Numbers like these are both exciting and troubling. How do we understand this? I'd like to first explore some of the "in your face" issues just revealed, then, as chapters unfold, tackle the larger spread of aftereffects and the impact they can have—lifelong.

INTUITIVE/PSYCHIC ABILITIES

Admit it. This is such a big issue that it's almost as if we all must have "gifts of the spirit" as part of our makeup as human beings—part of our

DNA—or else these percentages simply could not be that high. Fact: *the paranormal is normal for children*. That's *all* children. For those whose development was interrupted by medical crises, accidents, fetal distress, premature birth, abuse, the missing twin phenomenon, or a host of "interferences" that can and do occur in the womb, at birth, or as an infant, toddler, or little one—nine chances out of ten those children will either have a near-death experience or a near-death-like experience (not really that close to actual death but still in some type of similar threat/crisis). And they almost immediately begin to see spirits—everywhere—or dead grandparents who come to help out or a deceased pet who starts licking their nose. They hear things, see things, know things, feel things, and smell things no one should. I found this to be true in my first study with children, and, with about two-thirds of the adult experiencers in my research base. Count on it. The bizarre will somehow intrude when life is at risk. What impresses me, though, is that once this "door" has been opened, chances are pretty high that such "special gifts" become lifelong extras.

Nancy (case 4). "I remember focusing on sounds—the sound of my mother sweeping the porch, the sound of my feet crushing small stones beneath my shoes while walking in the street. I remember the sound of butterflies fluttering around my head in my neighbor's garden. The roller skate key being inserted in my roller skates, the sound of chalk as I was drawing the hopscotch pattern in the alley where we lived. Sounds were very meaningful to me. I asked my friends if they could hear those sounds and they said no."

Vicky (case 24). "I remember I grew up feeling and believing and wondering why I had to live my life twice, once in my mind and then again in my body. The way I experienced time 'the first time around' during an experience was much more natural and comfortable, but when I experienced it the second time, time was much slower, sluggish. It made me feel like life in a body, life in the physical, was so boring—since I already knew what was going to happen."

Emmy (case 16). "I realized that maybe everyone doesn't dream with their dead mom a couple times a week, and why the dead love to walk through my bedroom. And wake me up at 3:50 or 4:50 am."

A few child experiencers become professional psychics afterward. Although not a part of this project, per se, the story of what happened to Lisa Campion gives us an example of what can happen and sometimes does. She states, "My near-death event involves my missing twin. He died in utero, maybe around 12 weeks. I can see a black vortex opening in the pink and red light of the womb. I perceive this black vortex like a cold, dark black hole that opens and my brother is sucked in. I am left alone, completely bereft. There is a cord, like the umbilical cord, that still connects us. I can talk to him through that cord, like talking to someone on a long-distance phone call. I was born psychic because of this. I could see spirits, angels, dead people, and I had my 'imaginary friend,' my brother William, as a constant companion. I believe that he volunteered to come with me, but not to stay. I remember a conversation before his passing. He told me that he came in with me to keep me company for a short time, and that his passing would give me the gifts I needed to complete my life's purpose."*

Lisa became a pro. The vast majority of child experiencers never do. Instead, such abilities are usually regarded as on par with any other ability, hardly paranormal or anything else that may seem "spooky." The extraordinary literally becomes the ordinary.

Some do tussle with these abilities, deny their presence until they can deny no more. Eventually such extras are accepted. Why? Results. They're

---

*Lisa Campion gave me permission to use her story. Because of William and what happened to her afterward, she became a professional psychic, intuitive healer, and radio host for Empower Radio.

usually right-on. Because these abilities can be linked to the birth event or the natural development of children as they learn what works and what doesn't, the idea of "special" is meaningless. Religious orders, holy books, or clerics that seek to strike fear in the heart of child experiencers and their parents can sometimes threaten. They succeed in their idea of "truth" only when real facts about near-death states are withheld. Classes, summer camps, and a wide range of books and CDs/DVDs* can make more of a difference in situations like this than any horror story from angry parents or fearful clerics. Don't forget, most of the Catholic saints had near-death experiences as young children. Check historical notes. Discover for yourself how many of the world's "greats" have the same or similar story, same pattern. (I'll cover some of this in a later chapter).

LOSS OF BONDING WITH PARENTS

This hugely important issue causes more grief and misunderstanding within the family unit than any other single aftereffect.

My research, both with the 277 and the 120, shows that birthers and kids up to three or four, maybe five, tend to lose most or all of their bonding with parents after a near-death experience. Instead of Mom and Dad, they bond to any of the various beings of love and light who exist on the other side of death's curtain. Yes, love for their parents can still exist, and be deep, but it's no longer primary. Siblings can seem like strangers; the family unit a joke. It is not at all unusual for such youngsters to search high and low, every room, in the closets,

---

*One of the best places I know of for healthy, positive instruction about intuitive/psychic abilities is the Association for Research and Enlightenment (A.R.E.). Their programs are based on readings from the psychic Edgar Cayce, one of the greatest seers to have lived and known as the "father of holistic health and healing." The organization offers a full range of programs, conferences, and books along with one of the best summer camps for kids. Another source is Nancy Baumgarten of the Profound Awareness Institute. Her work teaching children, even entire families, about intuitive/psychic skills is extraordinary. See the "Resources" section for A.R.E.'s and Nancy's contact information.

under the beds, in other people's homes should the family go visiting, doggedly hunting for "the bright ones" or "the people" from the other worlds who left them behind. (Note: a small child will not use the term *angel* on their own, unless previously exposed to the term.) This "search mode" can reach such a pitch that child experiencers often will blame themselves, thinking that they somehow caused the special beings to leave—like it's all their fault. Children think like this. Child experiencers once grown, however, tend to look back and see things a bit differently. They tend to see themselves as "just the odd one out," and finally admit: the reason they never fit the family is because they couldn't.

Penelope (case 87). "I gathered my few clothing items and placed them in a small suitcase. I made my bed with military precision. I prepared myself. I had a determination that things had to be very precise. I had to put a TV tray at the end of my bed. I had to get some kind of cloth to cover it. I needed very specific items on it. I went downstairs and got some silver pieces that my mother had—silver tray, vase, pair of salt and pepper shakers. I gathered what I could. I felt that I was finished, and that I was ready. The light was fading outside. I sat on the edge of my bed, shoes and coat on, waiting for the people to come. Waiting for them to come and get me. I tried to explain what happened when I died, how beautiful it was, and how I am loved and the people are coming for me and that is why I am packed and ready to go. Nobody believed me. They are coming—but they never came. I tried this again at the Anglican Church. I am excited about what will take place here. They will come and take me. People snickered. I burst out the door into the light and warmth of the sun expecting them to be there. They were not. I burst into tears. Tried again and again. The people never came."

Dorothy (case 83). "I was in such a hurry to be born, wound up with the wrong people. I became leery and distrustful of adults. Fought my parents and my life."

Lori (case 81). "I raised my parents, counseled them when they had a problem. When five, I stood on the pews in church, raised my arms, and became overcome by crying during hymns. Role reversal. I was the parent."

Ford (case 30). "I became the family's odd one, the black sheep among my two older sisters and younger brother—that became my life's central theme. I started asking questions about God, which was received with surprise and laughter. I was content to be left alone."

That role reversal thing, child experiencers parenting their parents, happens more often than you might think. Probably because they really do know more and have become rather independent because of this. If parents would just listen without judgment, encourage their children to talk, describe things, much pain and confusion could be avoided or alleviated.

EMPATHS

Any empath is misunderstood—while in their family unit, at school, with friends, everywhere. Think double for experiencers—doubly misunderstood. These kids feel everything, every emotion, every response, every action and reaction. Parties and gatherings, even the splash and joy of holiday fun, can drive them in search of hideaways—if not in their bedroom, then outside wherever they can "disappear" or fade. Animal friends are safe as most pick up on moods and understand kids who do the same thing. It's not that such children don't like others, don't love special events or parties or adventures. It's just that the moods of others, fluctuating body language, cacophonies of loud voices, can either scare them beyond the norm or actually make them physically ill. Granted, the average kid can be so affected and recover quickly, while recognizing the difference between okay and not okay.

But for empathic child experiencers, "duck and cover" becomes a daily safety routine. They don't have a choice of whether to care or not to care. Remember that the next time you watch your favorite TV show. Maybe the near-death child beside you can handle it and maybe not. Note: their instant rapport with animals, wild things, and those who hurt or are sad is legendary!

Nancy (case 4). "Everyone was busy doing whatever one does at picnics but I kept feeling drawn to the fawn. How beautiful she was! I started speaking to her slowly at first so I wouldn't frighten her as I approached her. There was no fear coming from her. I sat down on the moss under the large oak tree and kept talking softly. She came right to me and to my surprise, laid down beside me and put her head on my knees! No fooling!"

Georgina (case 116). "There are positives and negatives. The way I can explain things, it is an honor to be alive, spiritually bursting love. Negatively, even though I accepted my body with difficulties, I don't regret it [a premature birth then, starved of oxygen while strapped into an incubator, developed cerebral palsy]. The feeling of frustration and being misunderstood is very complicated for me to express to others. I already knew that my life was going to be interesting and challenging in many ways and knew what path I would follow. I know animals. Harvey, my hamster, was dying of cancer. As soon as I got home one day, he crawled up and planted a kiss, went down to my cradled arms, snuggled in the crotch of my elbow, with me stroking his coat, reassuring him about going to pet heaven. I comfort animals at end of their life. Not many minutes went by, Harvey passed away. I've been blessed to know the way animals respond, show thanks, snuggle up to me and pass peacefully."

Cindy (case 60). "My mother always described me as an 'odd child,' a 'barefoot bohemian.' I have suffered my whole life with bouts of depression. Found letters from when I was a teenager, apologizing to my mother for being sad. Not wanting to live. But petrified of death. Feeling 'caught between worlds.' Wondered why I thought and felt so much . . . at the time not knowing what an empath was."

"Physical empaths are people whose bodies are so porous they seem to 'catch' from others their illnesses, fatigue, and emotional symptoms. An empath's sensitivity is a gift, but in order to fully develop and manage it, they need to learn how to stop absorbing other people's stresses."[1] Wise words from Judith Orloff, M.D., a psychiatrist and empath. Since she is one herself, her book, *The Empath's Survival Guide,* is a good source of where to begin as an individual with this sensitivity, child or adult, and how to understand why others respond to empaths as they do.

HIGHLY INTELLIGENT

Prepare yourself for more numbers. Can't avoid them. Let's begin with the 277. I went after specifics then as per intelligence/learning/school because records or school notations were easier to attain, plus I spent as much time as I could with parents. The current batch of 120 is different in that they are adults looking back over a life lived to reexamine cause and effect. You may be surprised at what they discovered about themselves. First things first, though. Here's a breakdown:

Mind works different from before   84%
Significant enhancement of intellect   68%
Birth to age fifteen, tested on genius level, IQ score 150–160   48%
   **Subgroup, *only those under 6,* tested on genius level,
     IQ score 150–160   81%
   **Birth to fifteen months (especially dark light NDEs),
     IQ score begins at 180 (nearly all scored like this or
     higher when old enough to be tested)

Drawn to and highly proficient in math/science/history	93%
Later on professionally employed in math/science/history	25%
School: Easier after experience	34%
Harder after experience	23%
Rejected school discipline	30%

NOTE: School figures are partial as 43% claimed either to have blocked out school memories or just couldn't recall.

Did you notice this? The younger the child the greater the jump in IQ scores once they were able to take such tests, *especially* if they had a dark or black light experience. Only four kids had genetic markers, which may have explained such a jump. None of the rest did. Also, notice how it was for them in classrooms and with teachers. Easy? Only for a few.

A stunner for me, though, was this observation: *After their near-death experience, children's learning ability tended in most cases to reverse. Instead of continuing on with the normal developmental learning curve— from concrete learning (details) to abstract learning (concepts)—they returned to life as if immersed in broad conceptual reasoning styles and had to learn the concrete method as if from scratch. The learning curve had reversed!*

Here are some examples of how this reversal tended to manifest: tiny ones often were reading books and newspapers by two and a half or three years old, and some had their own library card shortly thereafter. (Don't forget, folks actually used libraries and had library cards not that many years ago.) It was not unusual for some four-year-olds to prefer the *Wall Street Journal* over other reading choices. Once in school, they tended to drive their teachers nuts. One case of mine involved a boy who drowned and had a near-death experience about halfway through the first grade. When he had recovered and was back in school, he was surprised to find everyone still reading "See spot run," in *Dick and Jane* when he had switched to Greek mythology. Disgusted by this, he stomped up to his teacher and demanded to know why the book *Robinson Crusoe* was ever written (an example of "conceptual abstract thinking"). This, with a first grader!?! Forget your reaction to him. Imagine his teacher's. He was promptly pulled out of first grade and put in an advanced class for special learners.

Toddlers and the very young who can abstract? No fooling—they can and they do.

Most of us do not learn to abstract until college—a few earlier. Can you imagine what it would be like for such kids to be back in regular school? They're totally, completely, irreversibly BORED SILLY! The majority know more than their teacher, more than their parents, more than their school mates. How do they handle this? As you might suppose, not well. I'll talk more about school in another chapter, but for now, flip back to the page you've just read and take another look at the percentages of those drawn to and highly proficient in math/science/history versus those who actually found employment in those fields. Dismal. Face facts here. How can you earn a "sheepskin" (a college or university degree) when you're not allowed to express, develop, or follow conceptual abstractions—the creative impulses and knowings you have? What happens to the genius so many child experiencers of near-death states return with? You're not going to like the answer. But before we tackle that, let's play catch-up with that second batch.

Of the 120, 75 percent were highly intelligent afterward, many to the point of genius—slightly higher than the previous group, yet still in range. The basic pattern I saw with the 277 (that list with all the numbers you just read), holds with this group too—except this group is far more diverse in cultural backgrounds, learning opportunities, and family challenges. In fact, when it comes to intelligence and how the brain and nervous system are affected by the powerful shift of a near-death experience, *there is virtually no appreciable difference between the two groups*. The only real divider is direction of view—looking back instead of forward. This shift in viewpoint between the two groups reveals far more than anyone could imagine, including me.

Penelope (case 87). "My father is very excited because I am telling them things that I shouldn't know. My father questions me to test me. Although I don't recall everything, I know that there were questions about religion, reincarnation, and the Buddha. My father brought books home to verify the things I was saying. I recall his excitement that I knew all these things. He feels he has a true genius on his hands. My mother is not so convinced and also asks me questions. I tell her things that I should have no way of knowing. She is more concerned about how I could know these things. I told them of future events and where this knowing may lead. I told them that people would really be interested in the information, but that in order to tell them, I would have to tell about what had happened to me. This upset them both very much and they couldn't understand why I would have to tell that part of the story. I remember this part was gone over again and again. This made my mother insist that it all be put away and denied. My father was willing to continue but mother could have no part of it. One day I was in my class doing arithmetic. The teacher had asked us to pick out all the even numbers in a sequence of one to fifty. Somehow I misunderstood what she had said and I started dividing all the numbers by two. I was going backwards from fifty and had gotten down into the twenties when I got confused as to why some of the numbers had leftovers. I raised my hand and the teacher came to see my work. She seemed very surprised, and asked if I could show her how I did it. I did a couple and she seemed very pleased."

Penelope tried to describe how she knew numbers and what she did with them as they danced around her and sometimes her sister. Her drawing shows these dancing games. You can easily sense how accuracy can emerge from the play of numerical rhythms within the vast lands of the human mind.

Penelope, synesthesia with numbers

Study this drawing. What you are actually seeing in the drawing above is a form of synesthesia, or multiple or conjoined sensing. Synesthesia is fairly common as an aftereffect of near-death states, whether the experiencer is a child, a teen, or an adult. Defined as a neurological condition associated with the limbic system of the brain (the seat of emotions, memories, senses/instincts), synesthesia in simple terms means "blended or multiple senses."* Penelope wasn't just good at

---

*A personal aside: I was born with synesthesia and discovered much to my surprise that I was the only kid in the first grade at my school who could see music, hear numbers, and smell color. Because of this, I was continuously punished for being a bad child. Many times I had to sit on a tall stool in front of the class wearing a conical hat that said "DUNCE" on it. I was also born with dyslexia. Between these two "oddities" and the bombing of Pearl Harbor (during WWII), which totally terrified me, I learned to never trust adults and to always find my own truth myself.

math. The limbic system in her brain had altered. She could engage in multiple ways *besides thinking* to reach her goal of solving math problems at school. Her teacher called in an expert to interview her about how she was getting such great scores. She was so embarrassed, actually frightened by him, that she was unable to describe how she danced with the numbers in her head to get the answers she needed.

About half of both groups in this study displayed or spoke of sensory blends. For example: buying a painting for how it sounds, touching a table and feeling where it came from, seeing all sides of a box of breakfast cereal including top and bottom without touching the box, hearing trees and plants talk by walking near them, smelling colors, and seeing music.

Speaking of blends, there's another one that can occur in the brain after a near-death experience, especially with kids, and that is how math and music tend to connect, blend, or seemingly fuse together after such an episode. The brain's center for math is located "next door" to its center for music. Observation: the majority of experiencers with intelligence enhancements also exhibited a sudden, deep appreciation of and desire for music, many learning to play an instrument—like a violin or piano. When I first discovered this link, I wrote article after article suggesting that if school districts wanted to produce better mathematicians, specifically physicists, they needed to offer music classes too. Think I got anywhere with those articles? Nope.

Added to what you've read thus far on *aftereffects* are electrical sensitivity and time slips.

Listen to **Nicole (case 25)** describe her sensitivity to anything electrical. "I am very sensitive to energy from others (both deceased and living entities), and have no personal energetic boundaries (even though I try to put up an energetic 'barrier.') I see sparks of blue light in the air frequently. I am extremely electro-magnetic sensitive and am constantly getting static shocks of things, blowing lightbulbs, draining phone batteries, and draining the memory on computers. I have extremely heightened senses, especially with regard to noise, temperature, light, and smell. I can't wear synthetic fabrics and was allergy prone as a child. I am artistic, and use to draw amazing pictures of nature as a toddler with intricate details. I always felt connected to animals and nature and frequently tried to communicate with my pets psychically. When I grew up, I either wanted to be a vet, astrophysicist, or an archaeologist. I have always 'known' what it is like to die. How the spirit leaves the body (from the chest/head and moves up at a 45-degree angle)."

Now listen to *Patricia (case 52)* as she describes time slips: "I have time slipped as far back as I can recall. A strange but familiar feeling would come over me and the air around me would seem to gel or thicken. Then I couldn't move, but would experience something that was about to happen, usually just a few minutes into the future. I actually got in trouble for doing it in class during the 2nd or 3rd grade, when I 'slipped' and heard the teacher tell us to open our books to a particular page. Several times the teacher saw me open my book *before* she spoke and interrogated me about it. When I couldn't explain how I'd done it, I was punished. After that, the 'slips' diminished somewhat, but continued." (Note that what Patricia calls "time slips" is virtually the same as what I came to call "future memory episodes." I wrote about this phenomenon in my book *Future Memory*.[2])

A fellow by the name of Michael called me a few weeks ago, too late to be in this study. Now a fifty-nine-year-old retired police officer, detective, and one of those actively involved in the 9/11 tragedy in New York City, he confessed to feeling different all his life. Never fit in. Recently he has been flooded with prebirth memories of floating in another space where he was in training to be an angel who could fly—so during his birth he could "shoot in like a star." Laugh if you will, but this man, a dedicated professional, cried like a babe. He was overcome by these memories. No, he wasn't on drugs; nor was alcohol involved. This current rash of memories he was having somehow made sense to him and explained his childhood.

Although the average adult takes seven to ten years to integrate their near-death experience, it takes the average child experiencer twenty to forty years, some even longer, to integrate theirs. Why so long? Keep reading.

NINE

A Question of Family

*I did not speak at all until I was 3 years old. When I did,
I asked for someone to pass the salt. When questioned by
my mother as to why I had not spoken before, I told her I
never had anything to say before.*

DAVE (CASE 50)

*J*f you remembered a world filled with a loving light that knew
you and the truth of your beingness, and then suddenly you're
pushed out, plunked down, wrapped up, and glared at—in ways and
manners that don't even compare with where you once were—how
would you feel?

Babes can fret once they make the discovery that "here" is not the
same as "there." Still, with loving attention most settle right in—even
though many knew before their birth what they were getting into. How
this goes depends on the parenting skills of Mom and Dad. Yet, what
parents know any of this? You follow the guidance of experts, family,
friends, instinct. A kid's a kid. Right?

If there was any problem with pregnancy, birth, or afterward, especially with a toddler or very young child, you may want to rethink the
obvious.

And here's why.

A child who has had a near-death experience will think differently and respond differently than anyone else in your family and, nine chances out of ten, *that child will see right through you.* Yes, they need guidance. Yes, they need parenting. Yes, they're odd. But if you're smart, you'll draw them out via your interest in them and your willingness to listen *without judgment,* and you'll engage them in conversation as if they were more mature. Treat them like any other kid and you'll have problems. Or, should I say, they'll have the problem—how to fit in when they can't.

What I just offered is complicated. Because this is so, we'll be taking a broad look at the many factors involved, beginning with family.

VARIATIONS OF THE FAMILY UNIT

BJ (case 114). "We were poverty stricken as a family. Dad moved a lot. Had three siblings. Didn't get along with any of them. I wasn't wanted, born disabled. Hardly any friends. Nearly eight years old when started talking. Some say I had the voice of a real winged angel. I had spiritual contacts."

Nicki (case 82). "When I ask a question the answer comes in an energy wind-wave pouring into the depths of my soul. I would catch people in lies or detail something they did that they didn't want anyone to notice. I once asked my parents if I was adopted or had a brother who died. The answer to both, no."

Juan (case 119). "I knew from the beginning that I was different and it didn't bother me. If we played games, my imaginary world would be extremely vivid. I talk to everything around me. I talk to my pillow, my individual body parts, organs, animals, plants . . . I even talk to my emotions. I love the spirit world. Everything makes sense over there. It's not as complicated as this world."

Korey (case 93). "I perceived the universe very differently than those around me. I could see the connections between things. Other people's problems seemed tiny and frail next to what I was seeing. Solutions and explanations seemed so obvious as to be comical. While others became wrapped up in the dramas of their lives, I became a bastion of logic and reason. This is another way of saying that nobody wanted to hear what I had to say."

Sandra (case 28). "My parents, who left me home alone frequently, when working or dancing and drinking on the weekends, would come and get me to go to eat afterwards. I was in the back seat of the car when I heard a voice say: 'Seek love, knowledge, understanding, and wisdom.' I asked my parents if they heard that and they ignored me. But it struck my heart and I looked up the words in the dictionary the next day."

Veronica (case 64). "I was different—going to an all Black school, trying to fit in to a culture that rates people on the basis of their complexion and how much money the family had. My dark skin and the fact that we were poor and living in the projects left me feeling like an outsider. I was beaten periodically by my grandfather whenever my grandmother was away. I felt he hated me and my mother—took his rage out on me."

Marianthi (case 53). "My mother, who loved me, was prone to bouts of violent and irrational moods, delivered beatings on me for slight or imagined provocations. I used to go out of my body when her punishments were too painful and my awareness watched her do it from a level near the ceiling. Sometimes I thought that since my existence made her so unhappy, I should not exist."

Kelly (case 84). "At the age of 18 months, my biological father began molesting me, not because he was a sexual predator, but because it was the only way he could control me. It was also a way for him to penalize my mother, who did not know until I was 13. He had tried to kill her and me several times and the courts still kept granting him partial custody. By the age of 4, I was being raped and sodomized by men that my father would sell me to for drugs and money."

Penelope (case 87). "My mother tells us the large old brick building surrounded by a very large yard and high chain-link fence is an orphanage, and she has decided to bring some of us there because she can't handle us anymore. The screams let loose in that vehicle were loud enough to penetrate the metal. There were a lot of panicked, pleading questions, a lot of tears. It was times like this that somehow I could stare her down."

Monica (case 103). "There were four or five of us sharing that bedroom on any given night, and after she would leave I would listen to a full hour of cruel verbal abuse from my deeply angry brother, assuring me I was the most ugly and disgusting, vile human being ever to set foot on earth."

Easily one-third of the experiencers in this study had happy lives with parents they adored, and with siblings they both loved and challenged. The only clue I could find that might account for such success is this: the parents were intrigued by their child's differences, enough to engage them in various ways of exploring their ideas. Even though hard times came and went, that ever-present "I'm here for you" turned out to be a deciding factor in their child's progress. There were some who claimed they were never understood, could never really say what they wanted to say, share what they saw or felt; yet there was so much love and caring within the family unit that nothing else mattered and they did okay regardless.

UNEXPECTED RESPONSES TO
AND WITHIN THE EPISODE

In my first study, I wrote of a young man I met from New Zealand who was deeply disturbed about his father's refusal to help him during his greatest need. He had died when very young of a high fever due to pneumonia. Some of his case is repeated here because I've run across similar situations between parent and child many times since.

The boy had disobeyed his parents about playing outside, overdoing it, when he had not sufficiently recovered from a previous illness. Confined to bed, alone, frightened, and guilt-ridden, he left his painfully hot body and went in search of help. He described "walking" through the house and seeing his father enter the front door. He ran to his father with arms outstretched, believing that help had been found. His father looked at him in the face, then ran right past him, ignoring his pleas. (The boy was invisible to his father, but no one knew that at the time.) He was heartbroken by what his father did and decided that, because of this, he wasn't good enough to be loved anymore. He never saw how panic-stricken his father was once the boy's lifeless body was discovered nor the heroic efforts made to save him. When he revived in the hospital, all he remembered was pleading for help and being refused. He withdrew from his family after that and remained estranged from his father for many years. No amount of counseling made any difference, until we spoke. Finally, he could understand what had happened to him and why, and forgive his father.

Hear this, everyone. *The out-of-body component to a near-death experience is so vivid and so real to a child that most are incapable of telling any difference between what they see and what anyone else can see.* Often, they grow up still wondering why parents or siblings or friends failed to respond to their needs and questions when asked. *The fact that they may have shifted to another aspect, phase, or vibration of consciousness, perhaps existed in another plane of reality, occurs to no one.*

Along the same line, a young girl virtually choked to death in the kitchen of her home when eating a frozen treat she came to call "a death pop." The kitchen scene is of herself, her mom and dad, and her kid brother. "My mother was screaming and shaking a kid upside down by the ankles. My father was leaning over helping her. My younger brother sat in a chair at the table, watching. I was so scared! Boy, that kid must have really been naughty. I would never be so bad as to make Mom shake and scream like that! She yelled my name. I cringed and was upset that maybe I had something to do with her anger."

The young girl was outside her body the whole time, standing in the dining room as she watched what was happening in the kitchen. Guilt from how her parents reacted prevented her from associating "the kid" she saw with herself. The kicker here is this: to the right of her mother's shoulder was an extra child that she unmistakably identified by name as her brother Michael, whom she could clearly see, even though her mother insists that this was impossible. Michael wasn't conceived until the following year![1]

Another of those cases jumbles together the idea of good and evil, a subject all children face. A young boy and his brother were given permission to splash around in a motel swimming pool while a cousin applied for work. As many youngsters do, both boys promptly headed for the deepest end. A crisis ensued. The young boy watched everything from a point high above the pool: his body and that of his brother were pulled to safety by a white woman—who suddenly appeared, rescued the two kids, then disappeared. Once home his mother told him to shut up before he could say a single word, then she whipped both boys for leaving the house. He tried again and again, for days, to tell her what had happened at the pool—leaving his body, seeing everything from far above, the mysterious white woman. Guilt and shame came to overlie the miracle of his experience, not because of his episode, per se, but because of the way his family treated him after he came home. Certainly his mother was worried about her children and, to that degree, her reaction was understandable. But would her son have turned out differently if she had let him speak? I ask that question because after the whipping, he didn't care anymore. Within the span of one year, he turned from a positive, studious, happy, thoughtful child into a sullen criminal who didn't give a damn about anything or anyone. A long litany of difficulties followed, beginning with a prison term at the age of nineteen for a parole violation. It would take some digging to determine if the boy, an African American, was the victim of racial prejudice. But it wouldn't take any digging at all to pinpoint the moment he underwent a personality change that radically altered his life for the worse.

I mentioned these three cases to help you see how complicated the love and caring in a family unit can be. Forget the idea of guilt/innocence. What we have here are ordinary, actually wonderful, caring people, who had absolutely no idea that what seemed to be the right action to take was actually the worst thing they could do.

RELATIONSHIP PUZZLES

Rf *(case 31)* said he had a good family but felt isolated, alone. *Patricia (case 52)* said her family members joked that she must be a changeling or an alien. *Tony (case 2)* wanted to run away daily. His father was ordained as a Baptist minister and was convinced Jesus was coming. Very depressing household; became homosexual. *Mimi (case 117)* saw her personal life as a film in advance, including her future. Disowned by her father, took her half a century to emerge from the trauma.

The following are typical for the majority of child experiencers: their looks and personalities tend to vary from those of their siblings; often they stand alone in their views and habits—even from parents; unseen worlds can be vivid to them, including a whole host of invisible inhabitants; few can handle the kind of trauma other people laugh at (in movies, on television, or at school); most are drawn to birds, animals, and nature, many to varied forms of music and art; they are easily "lost" within social interactions they do not understand. Often, you find sexual abuse, beatings, and angry outbursts (even from siblings) to be at the core of what child experiencers face.

Cindy (case 120). "Growing up was difficult. I always referred to my family as a group of people who did not know each other, and they decided to stay in this house because it provided food, clothing, and shelter. I never cried; looked at the soul of people."

Andrew (case 5). "My entire life I was always attracted to the spiritual things in life. I am transgendered, or two spirited as many Indian folks say. My bio-family rejected me. I was horribly abused, so I had to make a life for myself. I think one day they will come around. I forgive them."

Rita (case 13). "I had a very traumatic childhood after my near-death experience in the womb, and all the memories were recaptured in later years when I would regress to events with helpers, at workshops, or by myself. The way the events went in my childhood reinforced my direct connection with Source that happened in the womb. I never lost that."

Connie (case 104). "Yes, I ran away a few times as a child. It was a tumultuous household full of rage from my Mother. I respect and love her tremendously, but she had 5 kids all under the age of 7 and no money after she committed my Dad to an institution for paranoid schizophrenia. Brilliant mind. He was kind hearted and warm but unreliable."

Perhaps a way to understand this is, once again, by the numbers. Of the 120 in this study 44 percent felt foreign—like an alien, 56 percent had problems with depression, 52 percent preferred nature to social relationships, 58 percent bonded with animals/birds, 43 percent had trouble identifying boundaries between them and others, 44 percent were alienated from normal relationships/lonely, 46 percent were rejected by their family, 54 percent were alienated from their siblings, and 43 percent had to contend with violence and sexual abuse within the family unit.

THE REALITY OF SUICIDE

This is important and it's scary and it's really strange, strange in the sense that what we're looking at here are child near-death experiencers who, for the most part, had positive, uplifting episodes. Why would the thought of suicide even exist?

With my first group (the 277), 21 percent either tried suicide or were suicide prone after their episode. This so surprised me that I almost begged other researchers to take a deeper look when conducting their own studies. Surely I must wrong. No one responded. So I took a deeper look at what I had, interviewed more, and this is what I discovered: *A child does not look at suicide like an adult does. They have no concept of hurting their family or causing anyone grief. Their logic is quite different. When they were not breathing, they were in a beautiful place with loving people. Now that they're breathing again, that beautiful place with loving people is gone. Aha! The way to go back there, then, is to stop breathing.* And that's exactly what they tried to do. It wasn't until they were older that they realized stopping their breath was wrong. To go back, all they needed was to learn visualization techniques, and they could visit anytime they wished. The catch: don't stay there or go back too often; you have a job to do and that job is here living out the life you have now.

With my second group (the 120), 74 percent either tried suicide or were suicide prone. That means that most of those in this present study faced the ultimate specter of self-harm. This shocking figure runs contrary to all other studies (although, admittedly, my research style tends to draw out more in-depth material). Still, why? Here are some "maybes" to consider. MAYBE, because this is the most diverse group I've ever come across; only those more deeply affected were ever drawn to participate. MAYBE, because the first group was younger, with most of their life yet to come, the contrast with this group of those who have lived longer and can look back on a broader span of life experiences really does make a significant difference in how aftereffects are handled.

The three-year study I detail in this book is the first of its kind in near-death research to focus solely on the very youngest child experiencers. So, the question remains: How do we explain the 74 percent?

Maybe there's another maybe.

Take a good look at **A. H. (case 65),** who tried suicide several times. "I ran home crying and looked for a knife in the kitchen. My mother asked why I was looking for a knife, and I said I wanted to kill myself. I remember feeling bad enough to want to die. Later on, when in a fight with my boyfriend, I went to a motel to commit suicide. I took pills and began writing a note to my mother saying it wasn't her fault. I passed out and saw a vast field. I was taken by ambulance to the hospital. I left the hospital and never told anyone what I did."

And *Almut (case 1).* "I used to be very very lonely and hugely depressed. Lots of suicidal thoughts. Nightmares. I traveled 900 miles to be with the man who I thought loved me only to find out that he had a girl-friend. I nearly cut my throat with a huge kitchen knife. A TREE, a Sequoia tree in front of the house, saved my LIFE!"

Both of these experiencers physically did the deed. They are the only ones of that 74 percent who followed through and with near-fatal results. The rest, well, see what you think after reading some of their stories.

Clothilde (case 57). "I remember as a teen swallowing a bunch of pills with lots of alcohol, and waking up later with a weird sensation of numbness and disorientation. And I remember thinking at the time of taking the pills that I wasn't sure what would happen but I might die and then maybe it was meant to be. I didn't try it again."

Penny (case 33). "I didn't become suicidal until my sophomore year after four moves and different schools. I actually had planned it out and had taken my parent's gun and put it in my night stand. Through an intervention that still seems mystical to me, my plan was thwarted."

Janee (case 113). "I have felt enough psychic and soul pain for long enough that I asked God to take me. One time I told God I was going to lie down on my bed and empty out and stop struggling and trying to be in control and 'It' could take me. I lay there for 45 minutes and nothing happened. I started laughing at myself—so ludicrous. I guess it's not my time then, so, I got up and continued with my muddling through."

Gil (case 10). "I felt lonely and desperately wanted to go home. There I will be so happy to be free and the real me and receive all the love I need and deserve. I thought that if I do it for the right reason, then it's fine. So I went to the beach at night, my heart beating greatly, and I walked over and against the snapping waves. I almost drowned myself but at the last moment when I was upside down, I touched my finger on the sand below and managed to flip myself back again. When I got out, I suddenly felt a huge amount of joy and understood that I don't have to do this. I can do whatever I want and live the life I want—and so I was very happy and started fixing my life for the better. What kept me going was my belief that I'm here for others, to serve and love."

Warren (case 51). "I wasn't thinking of suicide as such, just wanting to be with grandma so she wouldn't be alone and so that connection we had with each other could continue. I had no idea what dying was, just knew that she was leaving. That concept of her being alone is what I questioned at the time, like any child would of that age."

MAYBE, just MAYBE, the real factor here concerns the abstract of "ideation"—the desire but not the energy to follow through—along with an inner guidance that makes plain: *You're here for a reason. Forget about hasty exits. They tire you out but get you nowhere.*

Young children feel everything as truth. Remember that.

TEN

Health Issues

My eyes and ears and nose are sensitive still. I was a sniffer child. I had to smell everything before I could eat it. I even wear sunglasses at night because of massive light rays.

SANDRA (CASE 28)

*D*iscovery: the health issues and precautions I once prepared for parents of child experiencers, *equally apply to those same child experiencers when they are grown and throughout their life* (adult experiencers can face these too). An updated review follows.

SPECIAL HEALTHCARE NEEDS FOR CHILD EXPERIENCERS WHILE YOUNG AND THROUGHOUT LIFE

Blood pressure. It is normal for most near-death experiencers to have a drop in blood pressure after their episode, while still being active, hale, and hearty. Not necessarily an alert when one is a child, this can become an issue in teen or adult years, as current medical opinion considers long-term low blood pressure a major factor in cases of chronic fatigue syndrome, and it is treated chemically. Alert your doctor about this, as it may not apply to you.

Light sensitivity. Children are shoved outside for the fresh air that promotes good health. But if the children are experiencers, and the school teacher or coach or parent forces them to practice or play in bright sunshine for long periods of time, day after day, results could be troublesome. Because of their unusual sensitivity to light, they could be subject to allergic reactions to bright sunshine or unusual states of fatigue followed by a weakening of the body's immune system. Exception: there are some who cannot get enough sunshine. As they age, though, they invariably return to some degree of light sensitivity.

Sound sensitivity. Peer pressure is hard on kids, especially teens. Types of music listened to along with decibel level can comprise the mark of allegiance as to whatever is "in." At dances, proms, parties, gatherings, even school-wide assemblies in an auditorium, sound blasts out from loudspeakers. For experiencers, any type of loud music or noise or sound can be painful—even injurious. This can continue throughout life, irrespective of age, and can account for having to learn how to "exit gracefully" in social settings, or wanting to leave. Most prefer the natural world and the sounds of nature.

Electrical sensitivity. Stories of lightbulbs popping, computer memory vanishing, watches not running, cars breaking down, television programs appearing when the set is not on, microphones and tape recorders suddenly smoking—*none of these are a joke.* Not only are all of these happenings quite real, but electrical sensitivity also applies to lightning storms, tornados, earthquakes, and nearby power stations (as well as electrical transmission poles and the new proliferation of cell phone towers) and touches on all forms of digital equipment, including cell phones, iPads, computers, and so on. On top of it all, electrical companies are now forcing customers to sign up for smart meters hooked up directly to the power company.

All of this runs counter to the health of an individual after a near-death experience—and throughout their life. Sensitivities, along with the health problems that can accompany them, can increase with age. Certain precautions can make this livable—like using sun-powered batteries instead of electrical/digital ones, moving away from power stations, becoming active with citizen groups to relocate cell phone towers, maybe paying a fee to keep home hookups safe.[1] The mind is powerful, so talk to your electronic "friends" and honor them. Even computers could use some love.

Decreased tolerance of pharmaceuticals. When a child is ill, he or she is rushed to the doctor or maybe an emergency room in a nearby hospital, where a shot is administered or pills are prescribed. This is standard procedure. But if the little one is a near-death experiencer and suddenly more sensitive, possibly even allergic, to the type of pharmaceuticals normally administered to a child of his or her weight and age, that treatment could be more dangerous than the illness. Because this is true, I believe that all doctors should, as part of their workup, ask if that child *or adult* ever had a near-death experience. If yes, they should cut dosages to the smallest amount possible, or switch entirely to homeopathic remedies. If used right, homeopathic medicines, maybe even herbs or vitamin/mineral combinations—along with exercise, healthy food, and activity that supports a creative life—offer the better option.[2] The older the experiencer, the more this is true.

Of the 120, 46 percent became highly allergic to pharmaceuticals, 37 percent had consistently poor health, 32 percent had continuing problems with regular allopathic healthcare (medical procedures), and 67 percent either couldn't sleep much or had sleep issues. Things like light, sound, and electricity (odors, too) became ongoing challenges.

The inability to sleep was often the result of a more active dream-life, changing color tones, and/or a mind that could explore other worlds, visit with etheric beings, and question almost every single little tiny thing about the life they must now lead—like it or not. Sleep can be a struggle when the world around you makes sense one day and not the next, when the people in your life don't match who you thought they were.

Know this: There is a major difference between how children (especially the very young) and adults handle near-death aftereffects.

Adults deal with changes afterward, and they need to find new reference points. They are challenged to redefine themselves and the life they live from another perspective and can make before-and-after comparisons.

Children, on the other hand, deal with the strangeness of the mismatch between what they encounter in the world around them and what they know and identify with. They are challenged to recognize the source of their uniqueness and accept the validity of what they have gained from the experience. What happened to them is the basis of all they know.

Adults integrate. Children compensate.

Herein lies the challenge of the child experiencer once adulthood is reached, and full maturity is right around the corner. I mentioned earlier in this book that it takes the average adult experiencer seven to ten years to integrate what happened to them. Then I said it takes the average child experiencer twenty to forty years, maybe even longer, to do the same thing. The *why* answer: it takes that long for them to realize that their choices in life don't have to match others around them, that they don't have to pretend, that they don't have to put up with less to be more. In the next two chapters, this type of *compensation* will be illustrated through the growing-up choices they had to make and where those choices led.

ELEVEN

School, Dating, Sex

Being a kid was kind of interesting.

JUAN (CASE 119)

Notice this: the typical child experiencer is a fast learner, surprisingly smart, bored with school, has a vivid imagination, and is incredibly creative—all while going in and out of depressive states, mostly because of difficulties at home and being bullied at school.

Hear the following voices. Really hear them. Three surprises follow related to this request, along with some things you need to know.

Marianthi (case 53). "I was often humiliated by grammar school teachers who accused me of cheating in my homework, or using adult help when I would spell or write a story or do a drawing they considered quite beyond my years. Whenever they tested me to repeat a similar feat in the classroom, I did it with no trouble. I never liked school. It did not teach me what I wanted to know."

Sandra (case 28). "I could mentally add numbers without end. This became a problem when I started junior high and the teacher required me to show my work. I couldn't. My mind did the math, fractions, etc. so quickly, I didn't know how, I just got the correct answer. I do love learning, and I read everything within sight, multiple books at a time, non-fiction. School was too limiting and the teachers couldn't answer my questions or direct me to search the answers."

Paul (case 6). "I have always had a feeling of superior knowledge, mainly historic and religious, and never needed to study much for these subjects in school—yet always came top of my class throughout the year. I infuriated my teachers by arguing with them on certain matters which I was convinced that I was right; and after all these years, I find that I really was right and they were wrong in most cases. As a child I was almost always afraid, and frequently bullied, and often beaten."

Carmen (case 11). "I was good at school. I became very versatile in languages. I love the French language, but I also speak English, Catalan, Creole, and a little Arabic. I like learning other cultures in our nowadays life but also in the past. When I speak, I try to be very clear and illustrate what I want to say with different words, not always the same."

Karen (case 92). "I used to see some luminous triangles, about 2 or 3 inches across, and maybe some other geometric figures too, which used to float in the air in front of me. These seemed to be a sort of teaching device and I would get various sorts of information from their changes of position and speed."

Marian (case 12). "School was hellish. I remember sitting in first grade with my hands folded on the desk thinking that I could not fathom what these kids' minds must be like that they didn't rise up screaming and declare this whole thing insane."

SURPRISE #1: Hearing what you read is a form of synesthesia. I hope among the things you just "heard" is that these folk were trying to find a place in school—not knowing they had acquired sensory blends of various types via their near-death experience. Their faculties of perception had been altered because of this; that's one of the reasons they couldn't fit in. Neither parents or teachers knew this. Nor could anyone warn anyone else.

Like Paul, *Jen (case 72)* speaks for the many when she talks about being bullied. "I was horribly bullied. I was different. Not a day went by when I was not shunned, made fun of, mocked, or avoided. I was also teased by neighborhood kids. I was a bookworm and happiest curled up reading any time of the day or night. When I was young, I often thought of running away. I kept a suitcase packed with my things in the closet for 'just in case.'"

A large majority of near-death kids in both my studies became readers early on—most preferring history and information on civilizations they personally identified with and ways of living that seemed somehow familiar.

SURPRISE #2: Did you notice how creative these folks were as kids? (And throughout most of their lives, I might add.) Their imagination tended to soar whenever they gazed out school windows or watched problems solve themselves as if ripples in the air. Seldom was "pretend" ever involved or needed. What no one knew at the time is that the *imaginal worlds were open to them.* They could see things and involve themselves in activities no one else could. Should they say anything, unpleasantness usually followed. Children who are hushed or embarrassed frequently, shrink inside.

SURPRISE #3: Did you notice how their mind worked? How they thought and what they thought about? Easily three-quarters of the child experiencers in *both* my studies displayed the characteristics pattern that matches that of gifted children.

Linda Kreger Silverman,* Ph.D., a psychologist and director of the Gifted Development Center in Denver, Colorado, and the founder and director of the Institute for the Study of Advanced Development

---

*See "Resources" for contact information.

in Westminster, Colorado, is a leader in the field, and she has for the second time given me permission to list what's typical with the children she has identified in her research. I say for the "second time," because I first presented this list in *The New Children and Near-Death Experiences*. I'm doing it again here because these traits, these characteristics, are as true this time as they were the first. No difference. This strongly suggests that children who undergo a near-death experience, especially the youngest of the young, come back with a different "brain pattern" than they might have had judging by what is known about their families of origin, siblings, and their family's history. This may also address possible alterations in DNA (a topic to be covered later on).

CHARACTERISTICS OF GIFTED CHILDREN

Note: Those traits that seldom fit most near-death children are in italics. Those that do not fit any I have studied are starred.

Gifted children often have unique learning styles; they learn in different ways than other children.

They learn at a faster pace. They solve problems rapidly.

They are usually developmentally advanced. They learn to talk, walk, read, etc., earlier than usual.

They may appear healthier, physically stronger, and better coordinated than their age-mates.

They are very curious and tend to ask complex questions.

They give complicated answers. Their detailed explanations show that they have greater depth of understanding of topics than their classmates.

They are quick to recognize relationships, even relationships that others do not see.

They organize information in new ways, creating new perspectives.

They often see many solutions to a problem.

Their thinking is more abstract than their classmates', involving hypothetical possibilities rather than present realities.*

They often see ambiguity in what appears to be factual information.

They have large vocabularies and tend to express themselves well.

They have unusually good memories.

They are natural leaders. They may initiate and organize activities for others.

They also enjoy working independently. They easily become absorbed in the mastery of skills.

They may prefer the company of older children and adults.

They may like to be best at everything and may refuse to participate in activities in which they might fail.

They are often perfectionists, becoming very upset if things don't turn out as they expect. Sometimes they compare themselves and their achievements to great persons they have read about rather than to others their own age.

They are not necessarily gifted in all areas.

They usually don't want their giftedness pointed out.

As I noted above, the italics are of my own making with this list and indicate deviation, not for all but most. As to starred traits, I just never found them. This is significant, as it indicates child experiencers tend to make room in their lives for others and have little if any need to be "number one."

This reminds me of some talks I had with Dr. Silverman, when she spoke of Kazimierz Dabrowski, a Polish psychologist and psychiatrist, and his theory of emotional development in the study of sensitive, non-aggressive, highly intelligent, creative individuals.* Using neurological

---

*Dabrowski wrote a monograph titled, "The Moral Sensitivity of Gifted Children and the Evolution of Society." You can obtain a copy from Dr. Linda Silverman (see "Resources"). Also request her rendition of Dabrowski's theory, which discusses his ideas about positive disintegration of psychological structures in favor of compassion, integrity, and altruism.

examination, he documented that creatively gifted individuals had more pronounced responses to various types of stimuli. He called this "over-excitability" and equated it to an abundance of physical energy, heightened senses, vivid imagination, intellectual curiosity and drive, and a deep capacity to care. The greater the strength of these traits, the greater the potential for an ethical, compassionate path in adulthood.

I can't say that all those in my two studies had the kind of extra energy Dabrowski describes—a number of them had to deal with continued health problems afterward and throughout their life. Still, I can say their hearts were right there, willing and able to work long hours and overtime to complete whatever needed doing. What they lacked in muscle they more than made up for in projects that helped others.

DATING

Those projects, getting involved in life, were important to them. But for the most part—dating was a huge puzzle. The common lament: "Why bother?" So many knew what was going to happen before it did, they said no before they gave yes a chance.

Alison (case 78). "I used to ride horses and was obsessed with science fiction (Isaac Asimov). I had friends but I am awkward in social situations, as I always feel like I am in the background just watching, and struggle with social cues. I started dating in the sixth grade. I get on best with people who are intense or overthinkers."

Audy (case 39). "I knew every time I saw a man if I should or should not be with him. I usually know how long a relationship will last."

Graham (case 29). "I didn't like school because I felt I was being assimilated/indoctrinated into a mad, selfish, corrupt world. Interestingly, I fell deeply in love with a girl in my class at school when

I was about nine, which brought me out of my first frightening experience with depression."

Robyn (case 75). "Relationships with boys were complicated . . . a mix between boredom because I knew what was going to happen, and disappointment because I was sometimes too nice, as I was with everyone. I think people believed I wasn't genuine because I was so positive and happy all the time. I hugged everybody."

Carol (case 45). "I became a cheerleader, yearbook editor, Sorority President, Prom Queen. I was popular and I dated a lot. I loved contrast, so I became a surfer girl and a hippie."

Did you notice the range of different responses here? In case you didn't, here are others that should clarify for you just why the issue of dating was so difficult.

Nathan (case 115) felt profoundly disconnected from others; ***Mimi (case 117)*** found dating a real bore; ***Joyce (case 110)*** was really challenged because of her dark brown skin and brown eyes, and always feeling out of place; ***Penelope (case 87)*** also felt awkward and confused, and, like Joyce, came from a very poor family; ***Mae (case 71)*** felt like an observer outside her body watching everything happen; ***Jen (case 72)*** dealt with so many night terrors she delayed dating until college.

If there was an overall pattern to dating and friends and being social with these children during their early years, I would say this: they tended to be loners. Their preferences: pets, farm animals, trees, gardens, ponds, parks, and critters. Many still interacted with the other side and had little interest in those who couldn't see what they could or didn't believe any of it.

Here are some interesting percentages: 31 percent were very social with many friends, 33 percent were happy and joyful at school and at home, 44 percent were alienated from relationships and very lonely,

33 percent excelled in sports, 33 percent excelled in art, and 24 percent were excellent at music/math *as if both were the same subject.*

SEX

Maybe making friends was a real challenge, yet a little over half of those in this study (61 percent) had no problem at all with sex.

Marianthi (case 53) has an interesting viewpoint. "I was much guided by the vision/teaching of my own conception where I was shown the bright-light intermingling of my parents. The understanding gained there showed me that in sex, people exchanged much of what each of them was at the building block level of their essence, and how each of them could be positively and negatively affected in ways they did not register at the time. Nearly forgotten ancient teachings mention it. I came across them later on in school, and was thrilled to know there had been people who understood sex without the repression imposed by cultures or religions, nor with the bizarre, fizzy lightness of the last few generations."

Did you catch that? Marianthi was "present" for her own conception. She wasn't the only one. Several, in both studies, talked about that special glow they saw around their parents when, while having sex, the child they would soon be was actually conceived. Those who saw that glow never forgot it. Flip back a bit to chapter 7 where I discussed this. A refresher in case you can't readily find it: scientists have now been able to prove, over and over again prove, beyond doubt prove, that there is a light flash that appears at the conception *of every living thing (plus a death flash when life expires).* So, don't toss out stories kids tell about seeing their own parents conceive an Earth body for them while engaged in intercourse.

"I was very sexually motivated," said *Marian (case 12),* "but could not feel much else than shame because of my upbringing—so was promiscuous in an attempt to 'find love.'"

Several experiencers, all female, were masturbating *before* the first grade and lots more throughout grade school. I was surprised at this because usually it's boys who masturbate early. Not in this study. The freest with sex as children were the females, even going on sex binges. Considering the difficult family situations many came from, maybe Marian is right about why: it was an attempt to "feel" loved. I offer this because so very many were raped or abused by fathers, uncles, brothers, trusted family friends—even mothers.

There are other reasons, though. Consider what ***Monica (case 103)*** had to say. "I became a hippie at birth because I was raised by my teenage sisters. It was sex this and zigzag that. They resented being stuck with me and were none too gentle. I have eight sisters. The one closest to me in age and I got tossed into back seats and carted around like so much baggage."

All manner of sexual identity showed up in the early years: lesbian, homosexual, transgender, bisexual, virgin, sexless (claiming no gender). There were almost more boys than girls who chose virginity, with such a choice usually backed up by a strong identification with the spiritual and a feeling that God wanted them to be "pure" so healing and helping others would be paramount in their nature and life choices. I find it fascinating that the majority of those canonized as saints by the Catholic church had a near-death experience when very young; their devotional calling began as those just described.

Something worth noting: the older these kids became, the more independent they were. Unlike average youngsters, those who had a near-death experience when they were born or were a very small tike took off as soon as they could to explore what they could—even if that meant getting into trouble, yelled at, or punished. If they couldn't leave physically, they'd fly away mentally and spiritually to explore other dimensions of existence. Almost always they thought of others who they could help along the way. That's a trait they share in common. And here's another trait I haven't mentioned yet: One of the reasons some of these kids liked sex so much is because they often went out of body during sex acts and watched the whole thing from the ceiling or a high place looking down. Pleasurable feelings became even more pleasurable with the added fun of "watching" while "doing."

Dabrowski was right, though. Heightened senses, vivid imagination, intellectual curiosity and drive, and a deep capacity to care are all marks of children with a greater potential for an ethical, compassionate path in adulthood.

Did they achieve this as they aged? Not without bumps.

TWELVE

Growing Up, Jobs, Marriage

There is dark in the light and light in the darkness.

CAROL (CASE 41)

*A*strong sense of independence best describes experiencers during their growing up years—and that happened with or without parental approval.

Nancy (case 4) is a good example of this. "I was a professional model while in school, and I was a winner of over 32 beauty contests, did television commercials, magazine work, and so on. I learned from my friends that boys were afraid to ask me out for a date because of 'who' I was. They thought they would never have a chance to go out with me, so they never asked me for fear that I would turn them down."

So is *Tiffany (case 118).* "I liked older men and did not like sports at all. I wanted the high life and discovered it when I was in my late teens and early twenties. I moved well in circles of successful people with brilliant minds, and had famous boyfriends. I could see into the future. My intuition was very strong. One man said, 'You are so young to be so eccentric.' Eccentric? I thought everyone thought and felt like I did."

That same independent streak shows up quite differently with these two.

While in college, *Jaidyn, Nila's son (case 47),* no longer trusted his "childhood self" and believed he must have imagined everything. His choice was to be a lawyer who questioned all evidence, including facts from his own life. Yet, he could not "turn off" his occasional ability to see dead people and his strange sensitivity to light. ***Linda (case 95)*** has two unusual sons. Oliver, a birther, possessed full knowledge on every level, had full control of his life, and knew the future by fourteen months of age. Daniel, her second baby, was a near carbon copy of Oliver—although he never had a near-death experience. Both boys had the same ability to physically affect their environment, and they had known each other *before birth.* Yet, once they reached the tween years (just before puberty), both reverted to the same behavior patterning of an average child.

Jaidyn chose to "turn off" what made him unique (or at least he tried). With Linda's boys, an unexpected reversion happened as if "on cue." The rest split off in directions you may find uncomfortable. I know they found it that way. None of what follows exaggerates a single thing.

ON THE QUESTION OF SUBSTANCE ABUSE

Fully one-third of the 120 experiencers of my second study ran out the door while still fairly young, never to return. They'd been beaten, ignored, mistreated, or misunderstood quite enough. The others experimented with how to exist where they were by creating something akin to a "time warp," where any household, any job, any lover, any marriage that seemed to be the best choice at the time—or what was expected of them—would be okay. Whether obvious or whispered, results led to some type of rebellion. It's like they "blew a cork"—literally—with 45 percent turning to alcohol abuse and 46 percent to drugs.

In my previous study, 33 percent engaged in alcohol abuse—*starting in the first grade!* The biggest reason given for this: they couldn't handle the constant pain or embarrassment of being laughed at or ignored by friends and family when they spoke of their "special" experience and what was still happening in their life because of it. Seeing ghosts, demons, and the dead and being highly sensitive/psychic eventually switched from being playful to becoming more trouble than it was worth, even scary. How to stop it? For the young, it meant grabbing whatever numbing agent they could find (just like their parents did when they wanted to "drown" their sorrows [kids emulate what they see]). My current study, then, mimics the previous one in this regard except that the percentage of those hiding how they really feel, using substance abuse as a cover, is much higher! Here are two examples:

Dorothy (case 83). "I was a rebellious youth, smoking cigarettes at 13, pretty much hooked on alcohol and marijuana while still in high school. I ran with the wildest group of friends I could find—largely in protest to the strict Catholic schooling my father insisted on."

Audy (case 39). "I was an insatiable alcoholic. My body was exhausted physically and emotionally. My anger was still inside me and I didn't know how to express it, as I had kept it bottled up for so long. I had let someone else's actions run my life and I hated myself for it."

ON THE QUESTION OF DEMONS

People are surprised when I mention that child experiencers of near-death states see, speak to, and deal with demons. They think I'm joking. Nope. It happens.

Marcella (case 27). "There, standing in the doorway, was a being made of 'blackness.' He was a 3D shape of a human body, but all blackness, within and without. As we are composed of muscle, bones, skin, he was composed of blackness. Only his eyes were red. He made no movement, and made no sound. As I looked over at him, our family dog began to growl and show his teeth at this being. A dream? Not the dog."

Monica (case 103). "I was being tormented and terrorized frequently by demons. In my search for healing I have visited exorcists and have had deliverance prayers said—which actually caused me more trouble—including several years of being physically assaulted by demons day and night on a continuous basis. I finally found relief from this torment with an interesting visit to a famous French priest, an exorcist, who diagnosed me as a medium. He taught me how to close the 'open doors' which were allowing the negative energies access to me. All the physical and mental attacks including my suicidal thoughts and tendencies stopped after this."

Karen (case 92) let a "witch girl" trick her at summer camp. "She pointed the feather and began to say various things in a drippingly vindictive voice, one of which I recall, was: 'You'll start to gain weight for no reason, and you'll get larger and larger, until you'll be as fat as a pig, and you'll never be able to lose it, no matter how hard you try. And boys won't ever want to date you because you're so fat, and no one will like you.'"

The witch girl frightened herself saying all of this, then claimed she never should have but only her grandmother could undo the curse. The predictions came true, but not because of any curse. Karen had suffered the sudden onset of a thyroid problem that would cause irreversible weight gain *before* she went to summer camp. This whole episode echoed "coincidence"—the idea of cause and effect either reversing the order of occurrence or happening as if one event. (Coincidence, by the way, becomes commonplace with all ages of those who undergo a near-death experience.)

Three of those in this study were born into homes where voodoo was practiced (one lived in the bayou of Louisiana). What they experienced in their near-death episode did not match the beliefs and rituals common to family members, especially their mothers. The kids never fit, yet could not escape. All three drifted away from voodoo, turning first to magick, then to the brighter, more loving realities of the spiritual world. As children and young adults, they endured many abuses—including sexual—plus the effects of extreme poverty. Depression was commonplace, along with lack of sleep. Always, though, the truth of love and angels and God, of forgiveness and caring, remained a steady source of guidance.

Who's the demon here, though? In nine of the cases I had for this study, *the mother tried to kill her baby afterward because she was afraid of the child.* These mothers were afraid of how unusual their baby was, how peculiar in the myriad abilities and talents they had, all of which were completely unlike anyone else in the family, even beyond the mother's ability to cope with, understand, or appreciate.

Think about this: in our quest to understand what happens to the kids, maybe we should also try to understand the shock of parents—or anyone else in the family—who are unprepared for any of this.

ON THE QUESTION OF COUNSELING

Carol (case 41), after much rebellion, discovered individual counseling, women's groups, and couples' therapy. Then she discovered meditation and the Buddhist principle of karma, in the sense of how people treat each other and why, the idea behind "what you sow, you reap." This enabled her to create a meaningful life by shedding light into dark places, a skill that led to her current role as "sacred activist"* and

---

*To pursue what Carol means by her current role as a "sacred activist," you can contact her directly. See "Resources" under "Wisnieski, Carol Jean" for her information.

educator—working with people in hospice, prisons, and on the streets. She feels she has come full circle.

Unlike Carol, not everyone had a good experience with counselors. Consider these numbers: 50 percent sought out counselors/therapists of some kind, 24 percent said that doing so turned out to be a waste of time, and a whopping 69 percent walked away from any such opportunity—for good. Of these, the majority claimed they received more help from psychics than psychiatrists. These folk spoke glowingly about their use of crystals, incense, candles, singing bowls, bells, and water gardens—whatever would quiet the mind and give them perspective. Common place also were success stories from those who came to practice meditation, yoga, and mindfulness and took how-to classes in centeredness, self-love, healing, and forgiveness.

I want to recognize here those who wound up on farms and ranches, carving out a new life for themselves unrelated to anything else they knew. And, I also want to recognize those who, once they took off, traveled to nation after nation, almost as if bouncing along in search of some group, some job, some charity, some crisis, where they could fill a need or find a "home." Especially Native American peoples or First Nation experiencers; they too felt that same need to find "home"— seldom ever in the lands of their ancestors, but "elsewhere."

Again and again I saw this and, in both of the studies, *that need, that urge, that deep, deep passionate, sometimes lonely drive to find HOME,* even if that meant traveling the world in search of "place" or staying where they were and learning how to fit back in—somehow. Child experiencers of near-death states will go to extraordinary lengths to search for home, buy a home, keep a home . . . as if subconsciously they are still trying to go back to where they came from—not as babies—but as those who were once kicked out of heaven and still want to go back. The loneliness they feel is for "another place" just beyond what they can find.

I feel most are unable to find the help they need from the

counseling/therapeutic community because the majority of professionals today are not trained in "transpersonal" perspectives, or the recognition and acceptance of spiritual realities. It's as if without the honoring of positive, uplifting points of view, experiencers "starve." This I suspect is the true cause of much rebellion and any need to numb feelings. That truth . . . the truth they knew before ever being born . . . remains a hunger they will "feed" one way or another, recognized for what it is or not.

Transpersonal counseling is finally receiving some nationwide recognition by health professionals as a way to successfully assist new types of clients. One group formed to meet this need is the American Center for the Integration of Spiritually Transformative Experiences (ACISTE).* Theirs is a peer group facilitator program, with both certification and mentorship requirements, and yearly conferences to keep everyone up to speed. What keeps this group uniquely helpful for those in need is that at their core is love and a deep understanding of those they wish to serve. Theirs is a grassroots philosophy of values and goals: many of their facilitators are experiencers themselves, now trained to help others.

ON THE QUESTION OF GUIDANCE

By almost all accounts, there exists within near-death experiencers an "inner knower," a voice or sense or feeling that someone or something cares, that no matter how rough anything gets there are alternatives—better ways. Their job? Ask-listen-do. It's the "doing" part that catches many. Other glitches? Impatience or hesitation.

Let's look at this situation in several ways.

To begin with, 76 percent have a "rock-solid" knowing that all

---

*See "Resources" for more information about the ACISTE and how you can either assist or benefit from their services.

life, them included, is inherently spiritual—possessed of a higher consciousness and a greater reality than the physical world that appears around them. The rest are pretty much there, too, at least in the sense of feeling a unique rhythm or a vibration of something greater, maybe a presence or a power not of this world. Some call that God. Others are uncomfortable with G-O-D, and find other ways to express that sense of "greaterness." These folks do not pack churches: only 27 percent stick with or follow a religious path. That's a pretty small number compared with the overall sense of spiritual values they have; and, I might add, a preference for silence or being out in nature rather than in an edifice of any type. Still (get ready for this), *one half of those in this study said they actually saw Jesus!*

PLEASE NOTE: not all who saw Jesus were Christian.

PLEASE NOTE: irrespective of background or country, they knew Jesus was Jesus when they saw him, and they knew him by name.

I don't know about you, but I think this is amazing!

Some comments from experiencers follow:

Tiffany (case 118). "I was constantly interested in God. Loved stories of girls who became saints. Prayed to God all the time. Had imaginary dogs, 12 or 13 of them. In church I insisted that nobody sit next to me. Needed to leave room for my dogs."

Deborah A. (case 79). "I discovered that I could go to a sanctuary place inside of myself whenever I wished. It was a specific location, always appearing and feeling the same. It was filled with tall grass and daisies blowing in a gentle breeze, and was bright and warmed by the light of the sun. Here, I was totally loved, felt complete safety, and danced and played, knowing nothing could touch me in this sacred protected place. When I went to this special field, I would always wake the next morning feeling so very happy, safe, and knowing that everything was okay."

Cindy (case 120). "I am Hispanic. Born into a family of Hispanics, and I am the third generation. I remember the nuns in Catholic schools used terror tactics and yelled a lot. One day we were studying the Ten Commandments—it was all about hell-fire and brimstone. I quietly mentioned that God was not like that. The nun yelled at me. I saw her colors [aura] going off in all directions so I remained silent. Born legally blind, I have been protected by a committee of angels all my life."

Marcella (case 27). "There was no thing that was not Divine, and there were no 'things.' The 'I' that had been 'me' no longer existed. There was only 'SELF' in this Divine Eternal Light and Love—and that is All There Is. All form is Divine Light—no separate universes, no separate worlds, no separate nations, no separate people."

Georgia (case 8). "I have come to discover that a person can live in a pretty rarified space if they learn to really trust in God's grace the way the Disciples did. This isn't a religious notion alone, so much as a way to learn to listen to a different voice from that of the world, and to trust in that."

What is the number one way spiritual guidance was and is delivered? Dreams. Child experiencers pay attention to their dreams—often above all else. Dreams become as if a spiritual pathway, a door to that which is genuine. Along this line, 28 percent were inspired to become healers. A few made the commitment to move to a spiritual community and make their home there. The rest of them stayed with the rest of us.

JOBS

Be prepared to be amazed . . . 74 percent of near-death experiencers went on to have very successful careers—some in business, some in politics, some on farms and in churches, and some by making smart moves at the right time as if "guided." A number even became leaders of note.

As you might guess, becoming a minister turned out to be a popular choice. One achieved top union status operating a train on a popular commuter rail line. Another was once nominated for the Nobel Peace Prize for his work helping scores of those in need—then he went on to excel in the space industry, claiming that never in his life was he ever depressed. Many were teachers, authors, therapists, clinical psychologists, and social workers. The following are a few more specific cases:

> *Nancy (case 4)* became a top chemist.
> *Sister Rosemarie (case 37)* always knew from the start that she would become a nun.
> *Zoh (case 86)* became a holistic doctor, radio broadcaster, author, and television producer.
> *Kelly (case 84)* went on to become the first elected female county commissioner in her state.
> *Connie (case 104)* turned out to be gifted in handling investment properties and rentals, making a lot of money in the process.
> *Liliana (case 40)* ran a very popular dating service (she just "knew" who would make the best couples).

"Hear" some of their stories in their own words:

Reneé (case 80). "After fourteen years working behind the prison fence daily and enduring a prison riot, I transferred to Washington, D.C., as an assistant to the Education Administrator in Central Office. As a team we oversaw 114 federal prison schools where General Education Development (GED), vocational training, and English-as-a-Second-Language, law library, parenting education, employment skills, were taught. I was employed with the Federal Bureau of Prisons working nearly 21 years."

Dial (case 18). "I turned out to be a very successful business woman with DuPont for 15 years. Now, I manage my farm, Turtle Mountain Farm, with cows, donkeys, goats, and ducks. I've had a great life."

Lillian (case 56). "I co-founded a company in China, my partner and I, in one of the provinces—started commercial agriculture of cannabis hemp. Helped to redefine legal definition of cannabis versus hemp and received approval and permission from the Central Government. Currently over a million Chinese farmers cultivate hemp. Raised their disposable income from US$40 per harvest to US$100. This time my heart goes to medical cannabis. I strongly feel guided to bring this gifted plant from the Divine for medicine and healing to our world."

Joshua (case 69). "So I started my own tile company. I had to work out the back of a 4-door Chevy Corsica with a wet saw and all my tools. I did this for about a year before I could afford a van. After I got my first van, I saw first-hand how handy it is, and how much easier it is to haul tile around. My first van was a Dodge Caravan that I removed the seats out the back. After two years of struggling to find work, I hit the tipping point and got some good contractors that to this day still keep me very busy and pay me well. I have always been a positive thinker. We reap what we sow."

Karen (case 92) wants to be an inventor and has attended inventor groups. A lot of people have said her ideas are good ones. Although she lacks the money to proceed with her projects, she keeps trying. You see this spirit of invention, trying out something new to help others, with a lot of child experiencers. No matter the project, they keep moving forward until, like Josh, they fulfill their goals or find another that works out better. There's a knowing inside of them that just keeps on pushing.

Percentages here are very similar to my first study. Although 80 percent of them loved to work, their job history clearly did not address profit margins. What excited them was accomplishment—doing good.

With both groups some had serious money issues and lived in poverty. Even so, there was an uplifting attitude and sense of humor about them. Of those who participated in this study, one had barely enough money to buy the stamps she needed to send me her material (she never mentioned this until afterward). She did this to ensure her voice would be heard. It was. Another experiencer lost everything he had after achieving a windfall following the guidance he received. The reason he gave for this disaster? He claimed he got "the big head" and forgot how life really works. He wanted me to know this so I could warn others about being so stupid. I have.

MARRIAGE

Let's begin with Nancy, Nathan, Jeannie, Chester, and Jackie.

Nancy (case 4). "One day a new boy came to our school, a transfer from Hargrave Military Academy in Chatham, Virginia. Once I laid eyes on him, I fell in love instantly. One week later, he asked me to dance at our school dance and he fell in love with me instantly as well. We were together since that dance for over 50 years, until he died in 2012. It was a blessed marriage!"

Nathan (case 19). "Before meeting my wife I saw her years before in a dream, so when I actually met her, I knew we were going to pair up and spend some time together, have a family of our own. I even picked the name of our daughter before we got married."

Jeannie (case 23). "Love, sex, relationships were average until I met my husband. I have been with him since age 24. He was a man who could accept me for what/who I am. Never have had counseling of any type."

Chester (case 54). "Once I left home, the Seminary changed me a lot. I learned discipline and consideration there. I saw how chaotic home was. I was in Seminary for about 7 years. I left when I was 23 years old, and married my wife the next year. We now have 4 children and 8 grandchildren."

Jackie (case 62). "I was on track to becoming a nun. I was slow to mature physically, so I didn't do any real dating until college. I've been married for 36 years. It's been a good marriage. Though my husband can't relate to much of my spiritual side, he's very supportive. He has a strong spiritual self, too. It's just more mainstream than mine. I have two grown sons, fine young men with good spouses."

The numbers that follow are tricky, so have patience with me.

Let's start with the obvious: long-lasting marriages—first group 57 percent, this bunch 52 percent; divorces—first group 23 percent, this bunch 21 percent; never married—first group 20 percent, this bunch 25 percent. Not enough difference to matter, showing that whether "young in the game" or "long in the lens" wedded bliss was consistently good.

Really?

All those in the younger group gave a loud yes to that 57 percent, no exception. Yet those who were older, looking back, admitted otherwise. Only 31 percent of their marriages were actually happy ones. Complaints of being ignored or consistently misunderstood were the main reasons given for the difference; 18 percent dealt also with sexual abuse. The passing of many decades made a significant difference. What started out great ended up not so great.

I said the numbers here are tricky. Here's why I said that. Adult near-death experiencers have a massive divorce rate—77 to 80 percent split within five to ten years after their episode. This has confounded everyone. I bragged in my first study of the younger set that child experiencers once grown did just the opposite. Their marriages lasted because they didn't have the habits/baggage to contend with that adults did. Hah, was I ever wrong. Well, sort of.

What this study establishes is that the full pattern of aftereffects—physical, mental, emotional, spiritual—*has a far greater impact on both children and adults than anyone thought or that any research has shown.*

HOW THIS CAN AFFECT FAMILIES

Example: Psychic Abilities/Inner Knowing Often Extend Lifelong

Liliana (case 40). "When my oldest daughter was seven, I had a dream that I knew what was going to happen. Our stepfather was working in the jungle of Colombia for Texas Petroleum Company. In my dream, I saw how the helicopter he was going to go in went down in a thick forest. In my dream nobody was hurt but were almost eaten alive by mosquitoes. So I called the Company so that I may talk to my stepfather. They connected me with him by radio. I begged him not to take the helicopter that day, and he did not take it. Sure enough, the chopper fell. A day later they found the people in the helicopter alive, but they were bitten by many mosquitos."

Example: Best of Intentions Can Boomerang

Warren (case 51) finally recognized that ever since his near-death experience at age twenty-one months, he had done everything he could to help others. Becoming a school teacher put him in the position of handling racism straight on and working with those who had learning disabilities. Always respectful, he still wound up spending more time in other homes than his own, especially in Croatian orphanages and with Mexicans. Much of his strength came from prayer: "Every service in every church was holy to me." He later became a Baha'i. Pinched by a need for extra income, he started a business on the side, then went back to school for a higher degree. Exhaustion and a good psychologist helped him wake up:

aside from a heavy schedule, he was actually spending more time helping others than his own children, mainly his son. "I was neglectful," he said. This realization was both embarrassing to him and very depressing. Even hard to admit. Warren finally corrected the problem by scheduling his forays to assist others after first meeting the needs of his wife and children and his own need to spend time in prayer.

Warren's submission to this study, by the way, was the largest I received, a virtual book of his life story including family photos. He never had a moment throughout his long life to share his deepest thoughts. Once he could, he poured.

Example: The Aftermath of Near-Death Episodes
Can Haunt Experiencers

Leonard (case 49) died at the age of three, after being hit by a car as he was running after his uncle. He "came back" paralyzed and staring at the undercarriage of the car that had hit him. "I tried feverously to move my body but it just wouldn't work. All of a sudden, I heard an audible voice say, 'LET GO.' I still struggled to move. But again I heard, 'LET GO.' When I finally stopped fighting to move, I instantly felt what can only be described as a tingle (a pulsating, vibrational type of feeling). This pulsation would go from my feet to the top of my head, slow at first, then faster and faster, the cycle repeating itself. It was accompanied by a "woo-woo" sound. Then I found myself standing up. I can see buildings and houses but no cars. One major difference: everything looked like the negative of a photo—black or grayish and white. A figure across the street summoned me to come to her. I remember being a little scared about crossing the street as I might get struck again, but she assured me (not verbally, like mentally) that I would be OK. I just go over there and saw a picture of myself and two of my three brothers (the third wasn't born yet). Then another picture, and another, until I had images passing by me so fast that it became uncomfortable. Then a pause. I was now looking at a picture of a young man. He looked to be in his late teens or early twenties.

He had his arm around a girl that appeared to be the same age. As I am looking at this picture, I am struck by the realization that I am looking at my son. What? This is my son? I can't believe this is my son. I am just three years old! After it finished, I remember stepping into a dark cave or room. I remember feeling 'I shouldn't be here.' Then I felt a breeze and UNBELIEVABLE PEACE!"

While still holding the hand of the woman, Leonard turned and looked with amazement at the scene: the man who had hit him was bending over his paralyzed body. People were frantic; someone shouted, "Don't move him!" "I remember asking the lady what everyone was so worried about. I was more concerned with the feelings of those surrounding me than with my body lying there. A breeze hit me. I would say my intellect changed to that of a ten or fifteen year old after that." Much more happened to him. Finally rushed to a hospital, he began crying when his mother did. After fully recovering, he dismissed the strange out-of-body scene, the woman, the dark cave, and differences with time. When older, while trolling the Internet, he discovered a video of a near-death experience that helped him to realize something like that had happened to him. "I instantly went from someone who doubted these people to being one of these people." Faced with serious aneurism surgery, he prayed that it would all go away. As doctors prepared Leonard for surgery, the situation took a surprising turn. No aneurism. It disappeared. He walked away healed.

Again he searched the Internet, this time for an old girlfriend. She had told him she might be pregnant just before he and his parents moved away. He wondered about that even though many years had passed. He did locate a young man with the woman's last name and from the same town where he had once lived. After contacting him, he learned that the young man's mother was indeed Leonard's former girlfriend. She died when the boy was only ten. He sent three photos: the third was *exactly* the same one Leonard saw at the age of three when he was hit by a car and virtually killed.

THE EXPERIENCER'S CHILDREN

The first group were mostly either children at the time of their near-death event or young adults (a few were middle-aged). No statistics for them—at least nothing usable. The majority of the second group did indeed have children, averaging about two apiece. A few had large families and even larger numbers of grandchildren. Those who had no children: 42 percent. As near as I can tell most of the parents were successful with parenting skills. Where I found conflict, even resentment and anger, and siblings who could not get along was in those households where the parents themselves either couldn't stand each other, or the experiencer (usually female) simply hung on and on and on.

Absolutely startling, though, is evidence of Lamarckism.

I've run across this before—with children of adult experiencers *and* children of child experiencers once grown. It's as if that second generation was born with the same traits their parents had *acquired*. No DNA here; the word is *acquired*. What am I talking about? Here's the scoop.

Back in the late 1700s/early 1800s, a French biologist by the name of Jean-Baptiste Lamarck, made an interesting discovery: an organism can pass on characteristics that it has acquired during a lifetime to its offspring. Heavily criticized at the time, compelling evidence today shows that Lamarck knew what he was talking about.* This means that *memories and abilities gained in a person's near-death experience can be passed on to that person's children at conception.* These acquired traits

---

*What we know now from Lamarck's work is that "experiences of a parent, even before conceiving, markedly influence both structure and function in the nervous system of subsequent generations." Sometimes called "transgenerational epigenetic inheritance," the point here is that all types of influences that the parent's life experiences can cover—drug use, exposure to certain environments, even physical trauma—can be passed on at conception to future generations. This includes life-changing events such as a near-death experience and other types of transformations of consciousness. See "Genetic Memory Is the Key to Finding Evidence of Past Lives, Scientists Claim," posted on the Galactic Connection website on November 5, 2017, for more information.

(sometimes referred to as "transgenerational responses") are now being taken seriously.

Let me update this somewhat. In my own work I found that the more intense the near-death experience, the more likely traits acquired from it will show up in the next generation—and the one after that.

This is BIG! Not only does it confirm that near-death aftereffects can change one's life in significant ways, it also shows that generations to come can also be altered—just because of what happened to the parent.

Consider these comments:

Sandra (case 28). "Mine are amazing. All are multiply talented and the first two were determined 'both brained' on psychological tests at school. They are each interested and accomplished in all areas. The eldest started university at 15 years and graduated in four years with music pedagogy degree; the second at 14 in university, graduated at 19 as a chemical engineer. Both worked a couple of jobs in their fields, the entire time while also playing sports. They were all home educated. The last two were not given the IQ-type testing, as their sisters were before I took them out of school. All are amazing adults now with children."

Jackie (case 62). "When my second son was barely three years old, I asked him what he remembered about that moment he was born. He replied: 'It was tight.' He also mentioned at age four, that he and Jesus had been playing in the garden together. When I asked him what they were doing, he said: 'Just digging.' On another occasion, I woke hearing beautiful angels singing. No specific words, just a lovely sound. I got up to go into the other room and passed by my son's bed. He (age 4 or 5) popped up and said, 'Mom, did you hear the angels sing?'"

Vicky (case 24). "My son had started displaying psychic ability as a toddler, and from the ages of 4 to 7, he was able to see and hear the previous owners of our house, a man and woman in their 80s, talking to him."

Cara (case 14). "My sons have always been very aware. My younger son at 4 years old saw a dead bird on the road and asked me where the other part of the bird was. The three of us have been able to communicate without words. My younger son knows when someone is lying to him. We had many difficult school years because he didn't trust or listen to most teachers or administrators. I had to tell him he could call me at any time and I would take him out of school, no questions asked. We talked about situations that came up and looked for the best solution. At a young age my sons understood the big picture without being told. They watched what was happening around them, often making decisions in a more objective way. Both boys have had a great deal of fortitude from a young age helping others and animals, even when they were picked on by adults for stepping up. They also brought kids who were having a hard time in their life to the house and left them with me. They had a lot of poise for youngsters and had to learn to grow into their personal power."

THIRTEEN

PTSD and NDEs

I always felt/feel that I'm different from other people. I've even apologized to my adult daughter that I was sorry I couldn't seem to be a "normal" dad.

TONY (CASE 2)

*I*n the first group, 34 percent were positive about having had a near-death experience, 61 percent were negative.

What?

Almost in concert the answer they gave for this was: *growing up and finding their place in life was just too difficult.* The second group differs only by having added years to figure things out.

Ford (case 30) is one of the very few experiencers I've encountered, either child or adult, to openly admit *years after* his episode: "I was terrified of death, thinking it was the end of everything I knew FOREVER!" Perhaps the reason for such gloom is that soon after his experience, he lost himself in a haze of drugs and alcohol to dampen the impact of the aftereffects he was going through.

Who admits something like this? Kids do.

What we think we know about the near-death phenomenon is seriously challenged by the youngest of the young. In this chapter, what very few people ever mention is finally tackled head-on. The link is

136

true: child experiencers do indeed display some aspects of post-traumatic stress disorder (PTSD).

Take a look at these:

Mimi (case 117). "My life with my parents is a horror story. It took me half a century to emerge. My father thought I was possessed by the devil (as a result of an NDE!!!). I started to scream when he was nearby. Every day, all the time. He wanted me to change into a docile Christian. By screaming how bad I was, that I should burn in hell, that I was worthless, that I was not his child but the devil's child . . . I lost bit by bit. After my 9th birthday, my spirit was more or less broken."

Damon (case 112). "I would for many years feel desolate. At the beach I would stare at the horizon wanting to be 'out there.' I really didn't and still don't want to be here. It's not home. I didn't feel connected to other children either. From a young age, I carried the weight of the world on my shoulders, very serious."

Veronica (case 64). "Growing up was difficult. I was being sexually molested by an adult cousin, who also lived at my grandparents' home. My mother would suddenly come get me from my grandparents and take me to live with her—often in the middle of the night. There was usually yelling and sometimes my mother brought the sheriff when she came to get me. It was very stressful. I became a sleep walker as a result of having my sleep interrupted in such a way."

You've already read stories similar to these that in essence say the same thing: it's rough out there.

Bruce Greyson, M.D., one of the longtime researchers in the field and a contributor to the book *The Science of Near-Death Experiences,* points out that near-deathers do show more symptoms of PTSD than survivors of close brushes with death that never had a near-death experience, yet *not* as many as those who dealt with clinical PTSD. He asserts:

> Some of the phenomenological features of NDEs are difficult to explain in terms of our current understanding of psychological or physiological processes. For example, experiencers sometimes report having viewed their bodies from a different point in space and are able to describe accurately what was going on around them while they were ostensibly unconscious, or that they perceived corroborated events occurring at a distance outside the range of their sense organs, including blind individuals who describe accurate visual perceptions during their NDEs.[1]

Please note that Dr. Greyson's comments apply overall. They are not targeted to any particular age group.

At this writing, the percentage of children in the United States that suffer trauma and depression is one out of eight. A *60 Minutes* news special on this was done by Oprah Winfrey and shown on CBS TV. Oprah featured SaintA* in the show—a new type of organization for traumatized kids. Quite remarkable. You can still view that show if you want. If you do, you will see for yourself that near-death kids don't quite fit the billing. As Dr. Greyson indicated, some PTSD symptoms apply but not the clinical kind.

When talking about PTSD, know that there are many symptoms a person may exhibit. Thanks to an article written by Hal Taylor titled "Emerging from PTSD,"[2] we have a brief list of what he discov-

---

*I call your attention to the work of Bruce Perry, M.D., Ph.D., who founded SaintA, a Catholic orphanage converted into a center where foster homes are found for orphaned, abandoned, neglected, and abused children. What they have done to retrain staff in a system that really makes a significant difference in people's lives is nothing short of miraculous. Because they use "trauma-informed" care, they are able to pull children out of PTSD. They teach never to say, "How do you feel?" but to always say, "What happened to you?" For more information on this topic see "Resources."

ered about himself that could give us an across-the-board look at the subject:

- Fear that is seldom ever quieted
- Inability to concentrate for extended periods without falling asleep
- Temper bordering on violent
- Inability to differentiate
- Self-blame if unable to reach goals or perform perfectly
- Inability to feel empathy

Sherry (case 66) was wondering herself about PTSD and set out to see if any of the characteristics might apply to her. She read *Complex PTSD: Surviving to Thriving; A Guide and Map for Recovering from Childhood Trauma* by Pete Walker[3] who, like Hal Taylor, wanted to take a long look at what happened to him as a child and what he could do to heal himself. Says Sherry about her reading: "I was struck at the 'death-like' experience many children suffer, and how closely that hit home for me. As a smart, creative, sensitive child, I was always trying to figure it all out, make sense of it, fix it, fix me, so that I would fit in and wouldn't be the target for being outside of the circle. But nothing worked. I began to realize over time that it would never be fixed and I would be doomed to be a family scapegoat and black sheep, even though I was innocent, kind, and shy. My attempts to fix and make myself perfect would never work. It took me even more time (47 years to be precise) to give up on them altogether and stop trying. I realize now the thing that took me the longest time to realize, they were just nasty people and would never change."

Of the professional therapists in this particular field, you'll have a hard time finding anyone more qualified that Steven R. Vazquez, Ph.D., to speak specifically about working with child experiencers of near-death states. He is a licensed professional counselor and marriage and family therapist who specializes in a new psychotherapy method he discovered called Emotional Transformation Therapy, or ETT.* He has had sessions with many and what follows is a general comment from him, followed by feedback from **Gayatri (case 88),** who was one of his clients.

Dr. Vazquez: "I find that some people with early NDEs have difficulty finding language for their experiences, so they draw from different sources to explain it. When the language was not there at the time of the event, they must draw from language learned in later life to explain it, although others seem to explain it quite clearly and it can be corroborated."

Gayatri: "The RUB is literally how do you integrate all of that reality down into the small limited systems of 3D human cage reality of these earthy belief systems that have no basis in higher divine truth. In other words, even if the childhood NDE isn't traumatic the re-entry into 3D human systems is, and a whole lot of 'coping survival mechanisms' get set up at a very early age just to swing with it here on Mother Gaia."

Something else—a deeper sense, knowing, or awareness—is almost always present with near-death experiencers, and that "deeperness" doesn't fit diagnosis. This is what separates NDEs from clinical PTSD.

Here's what Satwant K. Pasricha in the book, *Making Sense of Near-Death Experiences,* has to say. Oh, by the way, she's the former professor and chair of the National Institute of Mental Health and Neurosciences in Bangalore, India, and has the experience to back up her words: "The major point of differentiation from PTSD is that NDErs do not try to avoid frequent memories of NDEs, and the positive affect decreases the possibility of subsequent stress symptoms."[4]

---

*Stephen has authored three articles on the subject: *Emotional Transformation Therapy, Accelerated Ecological Psychotherapy,* and *Spiritually Transformative Psychotherapy.* See "Resources" for more information.

Links to PTSD turn around once we "look again" at the entire scope of what we're dealing with. Remember this as we refer back to *Tony (case 2)*, whose comments opened this chapter. After dealing with the trauma of being "different," he now admits, "I wanted to run away daily. To escape. And yes, I've made scenarios in my mind on ways to "off" myself without it appearing to be suicide. I've even picked out a tree to drive my beautiful Jaguar into as fast as I can. It's in a straight line at a curve that if I just kept going straight, I would hit it. But those are at times in the past when I was at my lowest. I don't have those thoughts so much anymore. However, I would still like to escape from it all and take a long wonderful vacation in the tropics—and I will someday."

Doesn't he now sound fairly grounded for someone who was nearly crushed for "being so different" growing up?

Constance (case 63) had a black light experience that occurred at age three after attending the funeral of her seventeen-month-old-sister—whom she knew at the time was her twin soul. The trauma of losing such a companion was so great, she collapsed, went into shock, and was mute and utterly lost for an entire year. "It was difficult for me as on the other side I had my sister and love, but on earth I had my body. At some point, I decided to come back because I felt I had a mission: To let people know that God's love is real. To be a voice for God's love."

Dial (case 18) offered: "As a Native American, I discovered the Red Road and knew I had discovered my truth. I had returned home. Mother Earth and the animals became my teachers. I thought about it all at age 28. I discovered at that time of my life that I could will myself to die. I was taken up and was asked by a voice, 'Look back, make sure this is what you want.' I looked back, looked around, and at hundreds of people, many I knew. I realized while looking around I could not find Love. At this point I was asked: 'Will you go back and teach Love?' I agreed."

Let me repeat what **Sandra (case 28)** said earlier in this book: "I have a vision/intense feeling in my mind, of myself as a young child begging God to let me come to earth! I can picture myself, not God. He just is! I begged and begged him to let me come. I said: 'I know I can show them how to love you! I will love them and they will know you! They need me!' Now here I am and it has actually been easy to keep my promise to love, even against many trials and failures, to 'save people.'"

What's "normal" here?

Bruce H. Lipton and Steve Bhaerman, authors of *Spontaneous Evolution: Our Positive Future (and a Way to Get There from Here)*, have a good idea, at least they think they do.

> Consider the sobering fact that during the first six years of life, most of our beliefs about ourselves and the world are formed and adopted into our subconscious quite passively, according to what we experience and observe—all before we have developed critical thinking faculties that would allow us to reject self-defeating notions before we adopt them as beliefs that then shape our thought and actions, and the kind of lives we lead.[5]

Well, they have a point, but . . .

What if the world around us does not match what we see, what we hear, what we touch, what we feel, what we know? Many of the children in this study were preverbal when they had their experience—*yet they had no problem whatsoever recognizing what was going on and why.* Many of the children in this study were abstracting before the first grade—*yet they had to deal with learning reversals at school and at home.* Many of the children in this study never knew or understood *what a human being is or how to be one.*

They tumbled through life with feelings of guilt or a sense of betrayal—neither of which had *anything* to do with their family, their home, their school, their jobs, growing up, sex or the lack of it, relationships, marriage, their own children, or becoming elders.

All of this disguises the real issue: IT'S ALL ABOUT HOME! Guilt for wanting to go back. Betrayal for feeling kicked out. Help them recognize just this, and the healing they need will follow. Symptoms/ diagnosis of PTSD *fail utterly* to recognize or address this. Look at these numbers: 76 percent became more spiritual afterward, 27 percent turned to religion, and 28 percent became healers.

Here's a list of what is *normal* for the majority of child experiencers:

- A sense of guidance
- Invisible beings that are sometimes visible
- Occasional knowledge of the future
- Greater than average intelligence
- Solutions to problems others don't have
- More psychic awareness than average
- Possible out-of-body travels
- Wisdom that usually increases with the years
- Cleverness
- Inventiveness
- A need to help others heal
- Involvement in social causes if they can remain in the background
- An ability to often see what others don't
- A sense of loneliness that challenges understanding
- A little too much generosity

Those whose aftereffects increased with time: 73 percent. Note: this continual enhancement held true regardless of age—even for those who had reached their 86th year.

I venture here to share what I've consistently noticed: the brains of the very youngest near-death experiencers are decidedly different. Same for experiencers at any age, yes indeed, but with the youngest of the young? Even more so!

Remember that from birth to fifteen months is when the actual wiring of the brain is determined and synapse formation increases twenty-fold, utilizing twice the energy of an adult brain. Between three and five years old is the time of temporal lobe development, when children explore and experiment with possible roles, future patterns, and continuity of environment. How this fits: The strongest evidence for genius that I have found with child near-death experiencers was with those who had episodes during or around birth and up to fifteen months of age. Also, most alien, fairy, and monster sightings *with typical children* usually occur between three to five years of age—the exact same time frame when most childhood cases of near-death experiences occur, as well as stunning spiritual/religious visions and remembrances of past-lives, other worlds.

Notice that all this happens before the first grade, which is the reason I avoided cases from six years on for this study. However, in my previous work I did take cases up to fifteen years old, and still, the bulk of what I found then mimics this study.

I believe that all of this—specifically what we have just discussed—is the reason why young children do not integrate near-death experiences as older kids, teens, and adults do. They compensate, adjust, ignore but according to what I've seen do not even begin the integration process until somewhere between twenty to forty years of age. Yes, many of them *imprint or bond to the other side.* But, and it's a big but, the job of any child in any society is to learn and grow. Anything that interferes with that job is tucked away, ignored, or forgotten. Sometimes the only way child experiencers can be recognized is the pattern of aftereffects they display . . . without knowing why.

Adults have greater autonomy and control. They can make the kinds of choices the average child cannot. About one-fourth of the adult experiencers I have had sessions with toss the whole thing off to a peculiar vision or hallucination or dream, and then go on their merry way, ignoring any hint that there might be aftereffects or that maybe they should have given what happened to them a little more attention.

For a child, every event is a big event, an important NOW kind of thing. It doesn't take long before they have invested a great deal of emotion and energy in addressing whatever occurred and at whatever age, irrespective of whether it was real or imagined, an internal or an external reality. A child quickly learns what is allowable and what isn't, what will be tolerated from them and what will not. Their defense is to punt: see what might happen should they say something "odd." Any kid will test you to see how you respond *before* they do things.

Any counselor, therapist, or psychologist needs to rethink before they tackle cases where their client had a near-death experience when very young. Those who trained in transpersonal techniques fare much better. We already know that experiencers claim to get more help from psychics than psychiatrists. Yet some psychiatrists have already made "the leap" to more holistic measures. One of these is Robert W. Alcorn, M.D. (board certified) author of *Healing Stories: My Journey from Mainstream Psychiatry Toward Spiritual Healing,* who now uses shamanic spiritual interventions in his practice including "soul retrievals," the ancient shamanic skill of "mending" any damage to a person's soul and reuniting pieces that may be "missing." Some psychics now train in ways to use their intuition as a licensed therapist or medical clairvoyant. People like Winter Robinson, M.Ed., LCPC, author of *Hidden Order: Uncover Your Life's Design* and *Intuitions: Seeing with the Heart,* give workshops in such skills and the importance of ethics. Winter's reputation as both a therapist and an intuitive is stellar.*

Some child experiencers have great success trying other methods. ***Rita (case 13)*** is one of them. "When I re-experienced the first years of

---

*Winter Robinson, M.Ed., LCPC, along with workshops and personal counseling engagements, teaches the ethics of using intuition in therapy. See "Resources" for more information.

my life as a baby—this happened after a sexual kundalini experience—I experienced the way I worked with the cranial sacral fluid to comfort myself as a newborn as I was not receiving mothering, holding, mirroring from my mother, who was in a broken inner space of rage and deep pain from outer experiences."

Meditation and mindfulness make a huge difference for those willing to incorporate such practices into their lives. What I hear the most about from experiencers, though, is the spiritual practice of prayer. Thanks to Andrew Newberg, M.D. and Mark Robert Waldman, who wrote *How God Changes Your Brain: Breakthrough Findings from a Leading Neuroscientist,*[6] we now know scientifically how powerful prayer and spiritual practices really are—for all of us.

A BRIEF ASIDE—Researchers working with psychedelics have discovered that the drugs have a tendency to promote the growth of new brain cells, particularly those that reach out and forge connections with other brain cells, called "neural plasticity." The result is not only mind-expanding, but also emotionally uplifting. The goal here is finding new and better ways of treating depression and PTSD. What fascinates me with this is that near-death experiences are similar in effect and scope to psychedelics in that the brain expands. The difference, though, is that effects are lifelong and do not require the use of any such drugs.

Now, if we can just get to the point where we can handle the after-effects of near-death states better.

FOURTEEN

Solutions

In Bible school as a child we sang "I love to Tell the Story of Unseen Things Above." YES! This is my song! I know this is true!

ANN (CASE 91)

A powerful statement from ***Cara (case 14)*** began this book. It is more than appropriate to repeat the last three lines here: "Physical life is very small for me but my internal life is expansive. It is fascinating and difficult. Child experiencers have a great deal to share when viewed from another perspective."

That other perspective. . . that "other view," like what happened to Ann when she remembered a favorite childhood song. . . comes sooner or later in the form of a "wake-up call" that enables puzzle pieces to fall into place. Most of the experiencers in this study tackled the issue of "what next" on the way to more fully understanding what had happened to them and with a dogged determination to not only reinterpret the whys of their experience and their life but to literally break through into deeper realms of what is real and what isn't, what is Truth with a capital *T.* Simple solutions proved not to be that simple, as you will soon learn. Yet, what they discovered establishes that near-death experiences, and everything around and from them, defy pat answers. Experiencers do a good share of the talking in this chapter, so prepare yourself. Some of what they say will thrill you, shock you, stun you, challenge you, and/or reaffirm for you the importance of life and its living. What they share underscores the reality that no matter the conditions, positive or negative, a better way of living can be and is found.

To get us started, here are a few realizations some experiencers had. None of them are clear-cut, which may surprise you. Note that the italicized portions are of my own making, for emphasis.

Marilyn D. (case 76) came to know that *her future self was in fact her spirit guide.* "I sensed that an older woman had come to me and assured me that my life would be filled with joy once again. This wasn't a dream. I was wide awake. I could see her in my mind's eye. Suddenly it came to me that she was my future self as an older woman. My depression faded after that. Decades later, in my fifties during a meditation, I found myself talking to myself during that period of time when I was in that depression. It came to me that this was the 'me' who had talked to myself back then, as if I had just gone back in time."

Tamera (case 17). "Life was all that I set my gaze upon and survive I did. I describe that time in my life like this: on the one hand I was so grateful to experience life (it was explained to me—in the NDE—that it does not come without difficulties that I would have to just simply 'deal with'). I placed a black sheet over me (withdrew) and hid from all of my surroundings of childhood until the healing, renewing, loving times of life would return. *In essence, it feels to me now as an adult that I went into the darkness willfully that was of my own parents' making, and experienced it with them—compassionately, patiently.* In order so that I could maintain my perspective of love and not succumb to my environment's pressures to hate, be vindictive, or (even) totally give up."

Audy (case 39). "I started doing energy work and learned how to deal with what was going on inside of me. Instead of ignoring my emotions I faced them in their raw state, feeling each emotion fully. When I did that, I found they moved out of me quicker by acknowledging them. Whether people do these things intentionally or unintentionally does not matter. We don't know what others are suffering. Each of us experience it differently. *Holding onto hate and anger from the past causes more pain than good. It wasn't easy to let go and forgive, but when I did, that was when the true healing occurred.* I have learned so many valuable lessons from my drowning and from the path I took. I am truly grateful for them. Without them I would not understand myself or life as I do today. I will continue to learn and experience this beautiful life that has been given to me. From the ashes, I will come with a fire in my heart and passion in my soul."

Steve (case 38). "I had family problems age 21 that led me to despair, then suddenly WHAM! I found myself right in the center of that light I saw 16 years previously. *I now think religion is nonsense.* I translated the Bible from Greek, and it is clear that we have been lied to. *Our human beliefs hold us back.* My experience in light was definitely real, definitely real. We'll see a lot happen in the world in the coming years."

Rebecca (case 43). "Things happen to me that don't seem to happen to other people, or, if they do, they don't notice them. *My grown son said, 'Mom, does every anecdote have to end in you having a superpower?'* If you count infrared and ultraviolet and hearing the earth move (as I sit here I can hear the transponder that supplies electricity turning and turning, when it goes out, as it did a few years ago, it was excruciatingly loud), seeing red through my hand when a bird dies, lucid premonition dreams, synesthesia, knowing when someone is lying, feeling that my grandmother is dying and driving to her house to find her (as her doctor said) five minutes from death. Knowing the school is going to call that my child is sick before they call and arriving before they pick up the phone (giving some excuse as to why I was 'in the area' so I don't appear odd), on multiple occasions. And after each NDE [note: Rebecca was a multiple experiencer], if I was near a light bulb it would burst, my computer would die, the phones would go out, even my car engine went bad. After my sulfa experience I could, quite literally, hear conversations in another room and no one would believe me. I heard an emergency room nurse tell another that she was accepting a promotion, then go into another room and tell someone else that she felt bad about it because she was then moving back to her native country. I reported this to my doctor, and he still would not believe me! He could have verified this . . . in the ER. I identified a computer where the hard drive was going out because the noise was annoying me. It was so loud, the nurse said yes it was on the list to be replaced, and still no one believed me. *I guess too many of the things that happen to me do seem like superpowers. Try as I might, it's harder and harder to hide them. The older I get the less I want to.* As I'm sitting here typing this, I'm wrapped harder to hide them in a family quilt, that represents the fact that everything matters. There is a pattern and a reason to everything that happens in our lives. Every person, every contact, every 'where,' over time. We all matter. Take care in what you say, what you do, and how you show love. *It is all about love.*"

Their courage, their absolute knowing that solutions can be found to any problem, no matter dates or clocks applies to nearly 99 percent of the respondents in this study; similarly, to the first as well. The way out they find "within." No matter the extreme, no matter how devastating, or just plain quirky, these people follow a voice, urge, or light that simply won't go away. You see this with adult experiencers too, but not to the same extent as with child experiencers. Children take longer to deal with the challenge between what they absolutely know, and what exists in the worlds of people around them who couldn't care less what they know. Many experiencers feel this is the reason why kids take longer to integrate their episodes than do adults—*they need that extra time to learn, figure things out, then draw on that deeper sense of courage to step forward and claim their own kind of sanity in a world that barely sees or acknowledges them.*

Several cases I investigated utterly shatter any sense of reality anyone might have. They involved satanic cults, torture, demonic possession, and repeated rape—of small children and babies. How the victims survived is unbelievable enough; still, how they came to forgive and move on in positive loving ways is a lesson for us all. You've already heard from several throughout this book. I've held back the most dramatic because I wanted to give her a lot of space. Learning what she went through, and what it took for her to find solutions and to heal, will help us all.

First, Dr. Vazquez talks about another victim of "black magic" and the torture that goes on within such rituals. The individual he worked with had several near-death experiences.

I reviewed this woman's file. She had near-death experiences at four and again at seven. These "deaths" were reported to have occurred by means of a "black magic" ritual in which the child was killed. It is unclear how close to actual physical death this was, but she is convinced that something close to death occurred. She may also have mentioned a near-death around birth, but I do not have that in my notes. I have worked with several of similar cases of ritualistic abuse over the years. Torture is frequently used and perceived death or death threats often occur. Nobody knows for sure what actually happens in every case, but there is some evidence that this actually occurs in some cases. Memory of survivors has been questionable, but those who went through it are often very convinced of its veracity.[2]

Keep what Dr. Vazquez said in mind as I introduce you to *Judy (case 35).* She lived through seventeen near-death episodes, all of which occurred at various points in childhood beginning at six weeks of age. Much of what she went through is provable. The rest leaked out bit by bit as she tackled the scourge of alcoholism. Getting to the bottom of her addiction meant facing the dark secrets of her life. In her own words:

I was born into a family that for generations have been involved in a cult. They call themselves a satanic cult. Regardless, it is based in greed, drug trafficking, human trafficking, really whatever way they can do to find more power, money, and control. This is at every level of our government, religion, corporations, and business. This is not a conspiracy theory. My biological family whom I no longer have contact with once I remembered what had happened in my childhood, have been my greatest teachers.

I am now 61 years old, married for 40 years to an incredible man, and have three grown children and three grandchildren who are all the light and breath of my life. It's really quite amazing how the mind and body protects trauma until we are ready emotionally to allow the trauma to surface and be healed. I was 31 years old when I came into a recovery program, three months sober and drug free—I started to have flashbacks. First of sexual abuse, then of cult abuse. I had started using drugs when I was 13 years old. I did not know then my mother had been drugging me to forget the rituals from infancy. What I thought was my first experience was smoking pot. The next day, which was the first day of high school, I dropped acid. Immediate progression into other drugs, and absolute relief. Relief of what I didn't even have a clue. I continued my drug and alcohol use until I came to Alcohol Anonymous (AA). I now know the drug use probably saved my life. I was in a state of numbness most of my life. As I got older the drug use kept the pain down until I was ready. Miraculously, I was able to stop using drugs for all of my pregnancies, and as I raised my children. I had gotten down to smoking pot and drinking occasionally. My kids were 8, 6, and 3 when I went into recovery. My greatest motivation and guilt were for my children. Gratefully, and again it's a miracle, they will tell you they had a good childhood. They have their own journey in this life. I respect that completely. We are all very close as a family. Over my years of recovery, I encouraged each of them to seek therapy as well. They have in their adult years and are amazing human beings. All of my children are compassionate, loving, and kind. They are in jobs of service. They love to be of service. Of course they have had challenges along the way that were eventually embraced and transformed. We have incredible communication skills.

At three months sober the flashbacks started. From this point on it took 15 years in different types of therapy—Hypnosis, Gestalt—whatever and whoever I needed would show up in one way or another to help me heal.

Given the violent nature of the abuse and that it was on a consistent day-to-day basis, the mind is truly merciful to protect in this way. At one point, I was so exhausted of the non-stop flashbacks and memories coming so fast to be healed, I decided I was going to stop. I was so exhausted and tired of these memories consuming what felt like my entire life. I was raising three young children and working full time, something had to change. But it wasn't stopping therapy. Within six months I had a breakdown, was in hospital for three days, and decided to continue with therapy, and have never stopped since.

My mother is a high priestess. Although she's in her late 80s, she has no conscience, but hides it extremely well. So just to give a little background to why I had 17 NDEs and how the NDEs came to be a form of respite for me to survive, I was starved, beaten to death several times, poisoned, impregnated and aborted, held in a basement for eight months as an eight-year-old child, buried alive, and countless other rituals that had no end, ultimately to break me down with the threat of death constant. My mother aborted some of her pregnancies; they did that as part of their rituals, so I know she tried to abort me as well. My father spanked me so hard at six weeks to make me stop crying, the breath was knocked out of me and I hovered above my lifeless body in absolute love and peace. I was floating in a womb of blackness that felt like pure light. What brought me to tears as I was writing this now, was that I wasn't afraid or angry with him but had absolute love and compassion for how my father was in so much pain. I could feel his pain. I started to breathe on my own and came back to my body. My father committed suicide when I was 10.

As I was recovering and working through the memories, I was constantly questioning how I could have survived in this life. I now know I came into this life to shift the consciousness of my biological family and the members of the cult. I was shown that as they performed the rituals, I was in a protective bubble, and I could see that by being in my presence their heart chakra was ignited. What was dark before now ignited the eternal flame of their heart and their connection with the Divine Source. A remembrance, whether this changed them doing what they were doing, I don't know. I was also given the Grace of understanding how they were in so much darkness they truly could not remember "Who" they were. They needed my compassion, and the compassion flowed from me in that moment of realization. Truly a Gift that I, as a human being, really could not do on my own. I had an experience of our Oneness. Our apparent separation as them, as an abuser and myself as their victim, was revealed in that moment of Truth. I was not a victim. There was a purpose for those experiences. I have now been able to bring this awareness to my healing work and the clients who come to see me. This has been my greatest awareness and teaching. I was able to know Love, even in the darkness. Let me clarify, this does not mean I have a relationship with them. I do not condone what they do. I would never want to see them again, but I know the depths of their pain and can have compassion. God showed me this Truth each time I went "home" with each NDE. I would feel their pain. I had no judgment of what they did to me. I had the Grace of feeling Love flow through me as Truth was revealed. I cannot in words describe or portray how this felt, but that knowledge stayed with me. I had survived to see the Truth; there is no greater freedom. No more wasted time in resentment and self-pity. Those emotions were also valuable, but no longer necessary. I was ready for Truth.

Each of my grandchildren have been born Awake. They are amazing beings of Pure Love. Each one is kind and loving in an extraordinary way. It's quite remarkable. My husband and I have worked through so much and are best friends today. He has helped me most by loving me as I am with all the ups and downs. I am eternally grateful for him. He is my rock.

I have an incredible life today, strive to be open, and listen to how I can be of the greatest service. I am at times still triggered by things from my childhood, but look at that as another opportunity to heal at an even greater level. Because of the NDEs, I have no fear of dying. I know myself and I know the support and Grace I receive from all my Guides, Angels, and Beings walking this path with me. I am grateful for this lifetime and would not change any of it. There is freedom in knowing there are no victims. I am not a victim of my life in any way, no matter the "Experience." Today, I also know there are no mistakes. I needed to experience everything I did to be Who I Am today. My unique contribution to the bigger unknown, because I don't know what anything is for, I still have anxiety at times, another touchstone to know I need to dig deeper for the source of what that anxiety is covering up and needs to heal—allow every emotion to have expression. It has been a beautiful integration of my Human and Divine Selves. It's what we're doing in this intense energy and incredible time of Transformation. I am truly grateful to be alive at this time, and I know my presence makes a difference as do each of us, or we wouldn't be here. At 61 years I love my life. I know we as a collective consciousness are doing exactly what we are supposed to be doing. This is my freedom. This is Love. This is Truth.

Judy passes along to us this affirmation: "All of my experiences in this life, whether they appeared to be dark or light, are expressions of Love. Experiences of searching for Love. I came into this life with a purpose. This was not known to me until much later in my life, or I would not have been able to truly know the experiences as they were in the moment. What I know today has brought everything full circle."

Three more experiencers shared what they went through in their own quest for solutions.

Monica (case 103), still very much "in process," opened up her heart. "I have often asked myself, how is it that a creature such as I am, filled with grace and light, should be confined to the limitations of this humiliating human form? Stuck in time, I have only my senses, imagination, and intellect to navigate with. The suffering and the pleasures of life throw me again and again into spirals of darkness. So it is I have sought out the parameters of human possibility and so it is, ever so slowly, that *I am learning the importance of balance and moderation in the search for peace.*"

Alma (case 55) grapples with a second near-death experience later in her life. "It is so difficult to live in the present moment; I thought today and yesterday and the day before. *I feel so much since my recent episode, and have since my early childhood NDE. As you know, the reason it is so easy to lose our Light is because we are in most part raised by those with losing theirs, by yet another generation who was not taught to love themselves as God, as us, in us, living in us.* Our children today, who are allowed to shine, will be those who will reteach the rule of God

Supreme: we are divine and all Love and all Light into the Universes. My Light was dimmed as millions are/have been. We seek the Light in drugs, relationships, anywhere that does not hold pain. Or we drown in alcohol and other vices, just so that we further dim the greatness of our Light. *It is a large responsibility to be the Light of God. Yet this is our destiny, and Source NEVER makes mistakes.* We will continue until we all see that we are the Light of God, made manifest. For years I dimmed my Light to fit in with those already down trodden. After my more recent near-death experience, I will live my Light and expand my soul, and the very nature of being Love and Light."

Joshua (case 69) had a severe head wound at age five, almost six. In his experience he went to a dark place, like a vortex, with a vibration of "surrender." Once he did, everything expanded and enlarged, and many things happened. He was born left-handed, but because of his head injuries became right-handed and has a very high IQ. I spoke with his mother, and she remembered everything as if it were yesterday. Now in the construction business Josh shares what he learned from his experience with anyone who will listen. *To him, everything is a gift— something new will replace whatever is lost.* Sandra Champlain,* host of *We Don't Die Radio Show,* was so impressed with what he had learned from his experience that she asked him to be her guest for episode 137. His understanding of life continuously expands and is ongoing. "Treat everyone as if they were you, because they might be," he laughs.

All kinds of clever things happen when you are dealing with human DNA. We know through various scientific tests that you can wind or unwind it at will via thought and with intention. Examine details of Josh's healing and you see this, his determination not only to heal his very DNA but to learn everything he could about everything that

---

*Sandra is also the author of *We Don't Die: A Skeptic's Discovery of Life after Death.*

exists—and that means the human soul, who we are, and why we're here. Sandra gave him the opportunity to talk about this on her radio show. If you listen to it, what he says might "blow your mind." In that sense, much of what he has learned is no different from others in this study; Josh, though, got the opportunity to share "on the air."

MORE IDEAS AND SOLUTIONS

I've said this before to those who experienced a near-death episode, and I'll say it again: *Make your book!*

Regardless of whether you are a child or an adult, "you," the experiencer, will benefit in almost unbelievable ways if you write your story, put it on paper—not necessarily something that might be published, but for you; your book, your story. Get lots of paper, punch holes on the left for yarn or string to be inserted—something to hold your creation together. The first page is your cover. Name it; give your book a title and include you as the author. Then pour on pages that follow, write down every single detail. If you have news clips, tape them to pages in your book. Pour more. Say every little or big thing. Quote others who could bear witness, if possible. Keep on pouring. Put in pictures or drawings, poetry, questions, ideas, whatever pops into your mind. Pack it. This is your book. It is about your near-death experience. If you've had more than one, either expand your book or make two (or however many you need). *No one can validate your experience but you. This is the best how-to way I know.* So many do publish. That's fine. Just remember, your book is yours. Make it yours. Those I know who have done this say doing it, reading it, just having it around to touch or refer to once in a while was almost as life changing as their original experience.

You frequently hear of experiencers turning to a life of healing afterward, especially in regard to natural or more holistic methods; some become therapists or body workers, others turn to the ministry or take up psychic counseling. The theme of "service" predominates, even if they go the way of invention, scientific discoveries, business, farming.

Clothilde (case 57) wrote me a recent note. "I wanted to let you know, because of my experiences with death, in my family as well, from a young age, I am studying to become a thanadoula, to help people accept a peaceful transition out of their current life." (A thanadoula, in case you didn't know, is like a spiritual care coach/death midwife who accompanies dying individuals through their personal choices in the dying process.)

RESPECT FOR THE SOUL

Any solution that leads to success is grounded in respect for and acknowledgment of the "soul." Most experiencers define soul as "your Greater or Higher Self." God/Allah/Deity (whatever you call that Power) first, soul second.

The youngest of the young usually come back still in full accord with their soul. For them, their soul is ABSOLUTELY REAL. Not some appendage, or ghostly figure, or trick of the mind. The "who they are" connects with soul. Period. As they grow older, they may step back a bit and claim soul as guide, protector, friend, yet the idea of soul as one's personal link with "on High" remains. Not until they're repeatedly made fun of or bullied in school, does soul become a once-upon-a-time whisper. Although some never lose the realness of that connection, the majority do step out into society dedicated to whatever "growing up" may demand. As you've read in these pages, that connection to soul, their soul, never really diminished. Some just thought it did. Recovering one's place in the larger scheme of things is a valid part of the healing journey.

Irrespective of what soul really is, the issues of abortions, stillbirths, and miscarriages need a second look in light of what we already know.

Child experiencers make it very plain that the womb can still be inhabited from a previous pregnancy. Maybe the womb itself was never fully "cleaned out," or maybe the essence of whoever was there before still lingers. No one said this was a problem for them, but several indicated it was uncomfortable or "itchy" for a while.

In cases of twins, you can almost bet that the twin that died hangs around for a while. This can cause discord between the two, but most often the relationship between the living twin and the deceased other is more like a very good friendship that can continue even after birth. As previously mentioned, Elvis Presley is a good example of this—forever linked with his stillborn brother as if he were a "spirit friend" or protector.

Other cultures think differently about the idea of soul, the birthing process, and anything connected to near-death experiences. For instance, in this wonderful world of ours, there are teachings that claim the soul of a stillborn baby becomes the guide or guardian of its family, sharing that task with parents. Elements within near-death episodes in Asian cultures link to earth, while elements in Western episodes emphasize heaven.

The idea that "everyone in the family has an equal right to belong" is not only catching on within various types of therapy processes but is quickly becoming a mantra for handling the question of abortions and to what extent the woman has the right to choose. The best known of these new therapeutic practices is Hellinger's Family Constellations.* Now global in reach, this method helps to break destructive patterns in families and within family loyalties, including sessions that address the

---

*Family Constellations was developed in the 1990s by Bert Hellinger as an alternative therapeutic method that draws on elements of family systems therapy. It helps to break destructive family patterns of unhappiness, illness, failure, and addictions. Results are said to be immediate and life changing. Hellinger revolutionized the heart and soul of family therapy by illuminating the unconscious and often destructive patterns and loyalties. See "Resources" for more information.

souls of aborted and miscarried children. The recognition of soul by illuminating the unconscious is revolutionizing the heart and soul of family therapy.

The woman's right to choose abortion or pregnancy does not consider the rights of the soul. What emerges from Hellinger's Family Constellations and other forms of family therapy, *and from childhood near-death experiencers, especially the very youngest of the young,* is the absolute reality and validity of the human soul. From experiencers comes this suggestion: the woman is urged to first contact the soul of the unborn child she carries. This can be done through prayer, a hypnotic state, or while in reverie. The goal here is for the two souls (the woman and the unborn) to link their consciousness, so that the soul coming in can express itself. Does that soul want to be born under present conditions or is it willing to go elsewhere? Doing this, involving both souls in such an important decision, can ease or erase doubt/guilt.

Remember what I found in my previous study of children? One-third said they could see, hear, think, and understand around seven months in utero. I find this especially interesting because medical science tells us that during that same time frame, the preborn exhibit a full response to pain. Not only did this second study speak to that, the awarenesses these people claimed began before birth, during the entire time in the womb, and at birth.

I want to repeat here a case from that previous study. A daughter, once born and able to speak, accused her mother of trying to kill her. She "heard" her mother's thoughts during the time she was considering aborting the pregnancy. I spoke at length with the mother. She was consumed with guilt and said she had only considered abortion because she already had a number of children and could not afford another. She never carried through on her "thought," though. The daughter in utero "heard" her mother's thought about aborting her and panicked, fearing what she heard. When old enough to walk and speak, she pulled on her mother's skirt and asked her, "Why were you trying to kill me when I was in your tummy?" This case was fully verified by both parties.

Solutions require that first we honor ourselves, *the who and why we are,* and second that we make a commitment with our soul to awaken to the truth of whatever we find out about our past, this life, maybe previous ones, and then forgive everybody including ourselves. We celebrate the great notion of identity when we celebrate the fierce and wonderful realness of life and all that is connected with it.

FIFTEEN

Historical Cases

I have always known I have a mysterious purpose for being here.

NICKI (CASE 82)

hat effect might near-death experiences have had on history? Have any child experiencers, once matured, made a significant impact on society itself? I believe the answer is a GIANT HUGE YES!

Certainly no such phenomenon was ever noted in history per se, yet, what is recorded offers tantalizing hints that many of our revered historical figures may well have experienced near-death episodes in childhood that presaged their greatness.*

You already have a good sense of characteristics child experiencers often exhibit. When doing historical work, look for these additional clues:

- *A serious illness or accident between birth and five years, maybe up to fifteen years, that nearly claimed the individual's life.* Any record of an otherworldly vision or dream connected with the event that

---

*Some of the ongoing material comes from chapter 7, pages 123–132, of my book *The New Children and Near-Death Experiences.*

is considered highly unusual—be alert to whether he or she lived in a "primitive" social structure that honored spirits. How people handle things often depends on traditions in their culture. Be especially alert for anything to do with the mother's pregnancy, any womb issue, delivery problems, or birth trauma.

- *Marked differences in behavior afterward.* The child may be ahead of or different from age-mates for that historical period, becoming more so as the years advance, with a nontraditional or nonconformist attitude. He or she may have a charm or charisma that attracts people, animals, birds, etc. He or she could be considered socially retarded when young, yet unusually creative and bold, unafraid of death, highly intuitive, and aware of things future.

- *Presence of the cascade of aftereffects.* Although it is difficult to find existing records that register such characteristics, personal letters, journals, even poetry can reveal a great deal. Electrical sensitivity seldom applies, but a unique sensitivity to sun, sound, and the types of medication used at the time are often present. Note any excessive complaints about stomach upsets, numerous colds, or serious bouts with the flu. Even though experiencers are usually blessed with robust health, increased sensitivities, allergies, and occasional fits of depression may have made health issues a concern.

- *An almost obsessive drive to accomplish a particular task or project.* Most will have been workaholics with no sense of time or money, yet inclined to have property or be aligned with distinctive places or groups, whether or not they ever married.

Using these indicators, it is possible to find individuals back in history who so closely match the profile of aftereffects that it is extremely likely you will find an event in their childhood that could have led to a near-death experience. With Edward de Vere (the seventeenth Earl of Oxford), Albert Einstein, Abraham Lincoln, Black Elk, and Walter

Russell matches are so exact it's spooky. I cannot give full stories here, but in the next sections I do focus on those just mentioned because of the strangeness of their timelines. Others are noted as well, each of them equally fascinating and important.

FARTHER BACK IN HISTORY

Mary Anning (1799–1847). When fifteen months old, Anning was being held by a neighbor, who was standing with two other women under an elm tree watching a show put on by traveling horsemen, when lightning struck the tree—killing all three women. Onlookers rushed the infant home, where she revived in a bath of hot water. A local doctor declared her survival a miracle. Her family said she was sickly before the event but afterward really blossomed. Her curiosity, intelligence, and lively personality soared. She lived her entire life in Lyme Regis in Dorset County, England, where there are marine fossil beds on the cliffs along the English Channel. During winter landslides, she would collect fossils. She earned an income doing this. With very little education and snubbed because of her Congregational religion, she started writing articles on what she saw with the fossils, which had to be published by men who rarely gave her any credit for her ideas. It is thought that Charles Darwin read her articles. She excelled in geology, paleontology, and fossil collecting. Her many discoveries included famous or first-time skeletons of fish. In 2010, the Royal Society in England included Anning in a list of the ten British women who have most influenced the history of science. Today, she is considered a "now-famous scientist." (My thanks to Dan Punzak for this case.)

Edward de Vere, seventeenth Earl of Oxford (1550–1604). Born into the oldest noble family in England, tracing its roots to the time of William the Conqueror, de Vere's father, John, the sixteenth Earl, was late in years when his second wife delivered a son. Unusually bright as a child, Edward was seventh in line to the throne during the reign of Edward VI. Records show he may have had three near-death experiences during his lifetime. The first was at the age of twelve. His father suddenly collapsed and died; young Edward fell ill at the same time (perhaps by drinking from the same cup as his father—maybe poisoned—though this cannot be proved). He hung at the edge of death for several weeks (during this time the court made him a ward of Queen Elizabeth I in London). When he revived, he was plagued by recurring dreams and visions of his dead father and was told by him that he had been murdered. No one believed the boy's ghostly visitations. In two months his mother had remarried. Between coping with his own near-death, the corruption and political maneuverings of the queen's court at too early an age, not to mention his mother's remarriage, he sank into a deep depression. Here's what happened over the next few years:

- At age twelve he suddenly began to churn out compositions, publishing "Romeus and Juliet" under a pseudonym. Since noblemen of his rank never published, he was severely chastised.
- At age fourteen he graduated from college with a bachelor's degree, his college deans noting the incredible jump in his intelligence.
- Also at fourteen his first play, a tragicomedy, was performed at court. When he was between fourteen and seventeen, Queen Elizabeth seduced him (his poem "Venus and Adonis" is his version of the affair). He fell in love with the queen and with her wrote the words and music to "When I Was Fair and Young."
- At fifteen he learned that Leicester was also the queen's lover, a fact that overwhelmed him. He retreated into his study while haunted by dreams or visions of his dead father—they would go to "a cold gray place of mist" to talk. (Leicester was to become Claudius in *Hamlet*, Elizabeth would appear as Gertrude, and Burghley as Polonius.)
- At age sixteen he graduated with a master's degree, published

a number of student plays under names of which his guardian Burghley did not approve, then enrolled in law school.

- Also at age sixteen his capacity for learning accelerated even more; he read several dozen books per week in five languages (he owned hundreds of books himself, including the Geneva Bible that "Shakespeare" quoted from).

- At seventeen he was still the queen's lover but now accepted the secrecy demanded by her to maintain the "Virgin Queen" myth. He took up jousting and was unbeatable, and he had a reputation for being totally fearless and without any regard for death or his own safety.

- Also at age seventeen he published continuously and wrote dozens of pieces while at Gray's Inn (including a first draft of *Hamlet,* and the Robin Hood Quadrology in honor of his ancestor, King John being part two of that set). He accidentally killed a man sent to spy on him by his guardian, stabbing him through a curtain (the scene appears in his autobiography when Hamlet stabs Polonius through a curtain). He was found innocent in court.

- At age nineteen he was recruited by Walsingham into Elizabeth's espionage network and became a secret agent.

In case you haven't guessed by now, Edward de Vere is believed by many scholars to be the real Shakespeare. *All of the characters in Shakespeare's plays were people from Edward's own life.* He lived what he wrote about. *Hamlet* is his autobiography, point for point.*

By the way, Queen Elizabeth I (1533–1603) is also believed to be a child experiencer of a near-death state, dying young of a high fever then

---

*You can read more in-depth about his life, after what appear to be two more near-death experiences, in appendix 5 of my book *Future Memory*. I was assisted in gathering this material by Leslie Anne Dixon, a professional historian and expert on the subject. She had ten near-death experiences in her life, beginning at birth. And, yes, she is a genius. She has my forever thanks for all the help she gave me with this project.

suddenly displaying the now familiar pattern of aftereffects. With her, that jump in intelligence resulted in her wearing out every tutor brought in to educate her. Only Edward could match her intelligence, which is probably why they became close friends and lovers . . . for as long as possible.

Abraham Lincoln (1809–1865). When he was a child of five, Lincoln fell in a rain-swollen creek and drowned. His older friend, Austin Gollaher, grabbed his body, and, once ashore, "pounded on him in good earnest." Water poured from Lincoln's mouth as he thrashed back to consciousness. Although there is no record of the young boy's confiding an otherworldly journey to anyone, ample remarks were made by friends and family who observed his sudden craving for knowledge afterward, his insistence on learning to read, and his going to exhaustive lengths to consume every book he could find. Five years later, just after his mother's death and before his father remarried, he was on a wagon driving a horse and when he yelled, "Git up," the horse kicked him in the head. He hovered at death's door throughout the night, with his sister Sarah in attendance. On reviving, he completed the epithet aimed at the horse: ". . . you old hussy." Little can be gleaned about the incident until, as an adult, and referring to himself in the third person, he said: "A mystery of the human mind. In his tenth year, he was kicked by a horse, and apparently killed for a time."

Among the characteristics Lincoln came to exhibit: the loss of the fear of death, a love of music and solitude, unusual sensitivity to sound and light and food, sensing in multiples, wildly prolific psychic abilities, a preference for mysticism over religion, absorption tendencies (merging), dissociation (detachment), susceptibility to depression and moodiness, increased allergies, regular future memory episodes, hauntingly accurate visions, the ability to abstract and concentrate intensely, clustered thinking, charisma, moral upliftment, a brilliant mind, perseverance in the face of problems and obstacles, and a driving passion about his life's destiny. Certainly the argument can be made that Lincoln's many idiosyncrasies were the result of his extreme poverty as a youth coupled with a relentless determination to succeed. Yet nothing during his early years indicated genius; none of his unusual talents appeared until *after* he had survived two close brushes with death. As an adult, he nearly died again, and once more he displayed signs that he may have had yet another near-death episode—with additional aftereffects.

Albert Einstein (1879–1955). At the age of five Einstein nearly died of a serious illness. While still sick in bed, his father showed him a pocket compass. The fact that the iron needle always pointed in the same direction no matter how it was turned impressed him that something that exists in empty space must be influencing it. Although speech fluency did not occur until around the age of ten (perhaps because of dyslexia), family members recall how deeply he would reflect before answering any question—a trait that made him appear subnormal. Interestingly, he learned to play the violin at six (later delighting with the mathematical structure of music), taught himself calculus at fourteen, and enrolled in a university in Zurich, Switzerland, at fifteen. Like Lincoln, he was plagued with nervousness and stomach problems and nearly died from these afflictions as an adult. Also like Lincoln, the unusual characteristics of his temperament and talent trace back to the age of five and afterward.

J. Timothy Green, Ph.D., a fellow near-death researcher, has a fascinating notion as to how Einstein may have been inspired to produce a theory of relativity. He notes that Einstein was seventeen when he was a student of Albert von St. Gallen Heim, a distinguished professor of geology. Heim had once fallen while climbing the Alps and described a most peculiar death experience. Following this incident, he collected similar accounts over a twenty-five-year period from others who had fallen or had similar accidents. He presented conclusions to his research in 1892 and published his findings that same year. In so doing, Heim became the first person in modern history to publish a collection of what would later be referred to as near-death experiences. According to

Green, it is of record that Einstein was a student of Heim in the years immediately after the publication of this paper, and was privy to comments like: "When people fall from a great height, they often report that time seemed to slow down or stop completely, as it expands." Years later, when Einstein was interviewed as to how he came to work on the relativity theory, "He had been triggered off . . . by seeing a man falling from a Berlin rooftop. The man had survived with little injury. Einstein had run from his house. The man said that he had not felt the effects of gravity—a pronouncement that led to a new view of the universe."[1]

There is no question in my mind or in Green's (and he stated this to me) that it is important that these two men knew each other, and that Heim had an influence on the young Einstein. It is reasonable to suppose that the professor's near-death experience and his subsequent research paper on the subject had a profound effect on his curious student, laying the groundwork for Einstein's famous theory and maybe even validating what had previously happened to him as a lad of five. It is also well known that throughout his life he entered altered states of consciousness to rethink things. Calling them "thought experiments," he said a "storm" would sometimes go off in his brain as he thought through ideas, alternatives, and solutions.

Black Elk (1863–1950). Black Elk witnessed the Battle of Little Bighorn and participated in the Wounded Knee Massacre. But that's not why we know of him. He is famous because of a white man by the name of John Neihardt who interviewed him in 1930 and 1931, forever capturing his visions in the singular triumph, *Black Elk Speaks.*[2] His story: Black Elk began to hear voices and see spirit beings coming from the clouds at the age of five, but this confused him and caused many complications. At age nine, he fell seriously ill, his legs and arms swollen, his face puffed up. A disembodied voice spoke to him: "It is time Now, they are calling you." Two men appeared from out of the clouds, holding spears that flashed lightning.

"Hurry," he was told. "The Grandfathers want you." With that, he left his body behind and flew away into the cloud realms, joined by the men he "knew" were Thunder Beings. The imagery in this, a full-blown transcendent near-death experience, is among the most spectacular I have come across: flying horses, flaming arrows, forests, mountain peaks, cloud realms, explosions of color, beings of various types. Featured in his scenario are the Six Grandfathers (great powers), who taught him many things and both told and showed him his future, which would include hard times ahead for his people and special powers he would be given to help them. Then, his mission was revealed to him: he must *save the world* (a pretty tall order for a nine-year-old). Astride a bay horse and from high in the mountains, he gazed upon the world he was to save and saw more than he could tell and knew more than he could ever say. All knowledge was his. Beings he knew as the "riders of the four directions" came to him and he saw in a sacred manner the spirit shapes of all things, and he knew that all people must live together as one people. "And I saw the sacred hoop of my people was one of many hoops that made one circle, wide as daylight and as starlight. And in the center grew one mighty flowering tree to shelter all the children of one mother and one father, and I saw that it was holy." A spotted eagle took him back to his home and became a life-long "messenger" for him. "I could see my people's village far ahead, and I walked very fast, for I was homesick now. Then I saw my own tipi, and inside I saw my mother and my father bending over a sick boy that was myself. And as I entered the tipi someone was saying: 'The boy is coming to. You had better give him some water.' Then I was sitting up and I was sad because my mother and my father didn't seem to know I had been so far away." Black Elk remained as if half-dead for twelve more days. His experience replayed repeatedly in his mind, but he could not share it. If he tried, "It would be like a fog and get away from me." Too young to understand, he felt like he no longer belonged to his people. Feeling himself to be a stranger, he hardly ate and longed to be back in the spirit world.

Black Elk began to hear voices and have visions on a regular basis, including warnings of troubling times in the future. A medicine man recognized a powerful light coming from him. He seemed to levitate at age thirteen as he was prepared by his father for the Battle of Little Bighorn. By age seventeen, he was warned in a visitation from the Thunder Beings that a penalty of death by lightning would be meted out if he didn't share what had happened to him when he was nine. He finally told his story. Realizing that saving the world really meant healing people, he became a medicine man and began to heal the sick. Black Elk was very much aware that it was not he who cured people, but the Great Spirit. This humility lasted throughout his lifetime. Nearly blind when older, he became a recluse. His conversion to Christianity was a mere convenience, for he knew that God was the God of all. Biographers were discouraged from writing about him, as it was against federal law at that time for Indians to discuss the "old ways" or the religion of their past. John Neihardt, who was familiar with the Lakota Sioux and was accompanied by his interpreter, Flying Hawk, went in search of Black Elk. Why the old man was waiting for him as if he was expected and then broke federal law by trusting this white man and sharing with him his greatest vision is a mystery—until you know something about Neihardt. At the age of eleven, Neihardt had "died" of a high fever and had a dramatic near-death experience. Never the same again, he became like Black Elk—one of those who *know*. The recognition and camaraderie between the two were instantaneous, and they became as family. The book Neihardt wrote went out of print but was discovered by Carl Jung and republished in the sixties. It became a bestseller, hailed, even by Native Americans, as the Rosetta Stone of authentic Native American spirituality.

Walter Russell (1871–1963). Russell had his first near-death experience at age seven, and it prepared him in a strange way for the financial disaster his family would soon suffer. In 1881, at age ten, Russell was pulled from school and sent to work, keeping "a good heart" because of the unfailing faith he had gained from his otherworld journey when he was seven. A musician since infancy, he secured a church organist position at thirteen and became entirely self-supporting and self-educated after that, earning his way through five years of art school. When he was fourteen his plans were interrupted by black diphtheria and another near-death episode. He was pronounced dead by the attending physician. He claimed to have discovered the secret of healing during this event, as he felt he had entered "at-one-ment" with God. These two near-death experiences set the stage for dramatic periods of illumination that would occur every seven years throughout his life. Says Glenn Clark in his biography of Russell, *The Man Who Tapped the Secrets of the Universe*:

> He escaped encyclopedical educational systems of information-cramming and memory-testing which filled other children's lives until they were twenty-five. He used his precious youth to find out the secret mysteries of his inner Self. His whole life has been used in the search of the real Self and the relation of this real Self to the selective universe of which he knows himself to be a vital part.[3]

Russell excelled in whatever he turned a hand to and won lasting friendships and lucrative art commissions. He had a studio in Carnegie Hall in New York City, became a commissioned sculptor for President and Mrs. Franklin Delano Roosevelt, was a longtime friend of Mark Twain, and painted and sculpted Thomas Edison. Russell's motto was "Mediocrity is self-inflicted. Genius is self-bestowed." At age forty-nine, he suddenly was enveloped in a state of "cosmic consciousness." This state lasted for thirty-nine days and nights without abating.

> My personal reaction to this great happening left me wholly Mind, with but slight awareness of my electric body. During practically all of the time, I felt that my body was not a part of me but attached to

my Consciousness by electric threads of light. When I had to use my body in such acts as writing in words the essence of God's Message, it was extremely difficult to bring my body back under control.[4]

Once he regained use of his faculties, he set about recording the experience in *The Message of the Divine Iliad* and then spent six years penning *The Universal One*—a text containing the drawings and revelations given to him of the universe and how it worked, covering such subjects as chemistry, physics, and electromagnetics. He later corresponded with Albert Einstein about his own theory that this is a "thought-wave" universe created for the transmission of thought. His second and lasting marriage was to English-born Lao Russell, herself a visionary since childhood, who grew up knowing she was here "to change the thinking of the world." Together they established the University of Science and Philosophy.*

Edgar Cayce (1877–1945). Known as the "sleeping prophet," the "father of holistic medicine," and the most documented psychic in modern times, Cayce spent forty years of his adult life giving psychic "readings" to thousands of seekers while in an unconscious state, diagnosing illnesses and revealing lives lived in the distant past and prophecies yet to come. He had the ability to put himself in a sleeplike state by lying down on a couch, closing his eyes, and folding his hands over his stomach. In this state, he was able to place his mind in contact with all time and space—the universal consciousness—and respond to questions. Records of his readings help people even today. Best known for his prophecies, the majority of what he offered actually dealt more with holistic health and the treatment of illness. His readings from the A.R.E. cover 10,000 different topics. Information about records of his readings, research about them, and a host of classes, conferences,

---

*Although Walter and Lao have long since passed on, the university continues via its website, a new headquarters and museum in Waynesboro, Virginia, and tours through the place where they once lived. See "Resources" for more information.

and live-streaming events based on his work are available at A.R.E., a nonprofit organization founded in 1931 (see "Resources" for more information). Neil Helm, Scholar in Residence at Atlantic University (part of A.R.E.), himself a near-death experiencer, investigated stories that Edgar Cayce may have had a near-death experience as a youngster. He was able to trace letters written at the time that described a drowning when Cayce was about five, where he was pronounced dead. It was only after this incident that he began to have interactions with invisible playmates, experience out-of-body episodes, know what was in a book by sleeping on it, and manifest the beginnings of psychic gifts that did not fully develop until he was an adult. Only letters about this exist. Although not constituting proof, the pattern of Cayce's life matches what often occurs with child experiencers.

Marcel Vogel (1917–1991). Marcel Vogel suffered from respiratory difficulties and died at the age of six, officially pronounced dead of double lobar pneumonia. The impact of his "coming back," coupled with the experience he had, made life very difficult for him. He became a loner, overwhelmed by the light he saw when he died and the sense of love and well-being it gave him. Physical life, though, made no sense to him until he discovered the glow worms in the backyard of his family's vacation property. The light the little insects flashed on and off captured his fancy. During a walk to early Mass one morning, he asked in prayer: "Why am I here? What is the purpose of my life? Soon after, he heard a voice in his mind say, "You will be a phosphor chemist. You will do pioneering work in luminescence. You will write a book and create your own business." Can you imagine a six-year-old being told that?

He and his father, Joseph, built a laboratory in the back of their home and young Marcel set about attempting to duplicate the chemical that made fireflies in his backyard glow. At the age of twelve he had synthesized a chemical compound that when mixed in water with potassium ferrocyanide and hydrogen peroxide, produced a chemiluminescence that matched the light of the firefly. Then he converted ultraviolet radiation in the tube to visible form—visible light. While still in grade school, he visited the Mechanics Institute and translated, from German, the original articles on phosphor chemistry. Off and running, he quickly duplicated everything he learned at the Institute in his own amateur laboratory.

Vogel worked as a research scientist at IBM for twenty-seven years, earning thirty-two patents. Once retired he created Psychic Research, Inc. (his own lab and business). The book he wrote was *The Luminescence of Liquids and Solids and Their Practical Application.* The last seventeen years of his life he pioneered research into the relationship between quartz crystals and water. If you own a Vogel-cut crystal, consider it a rare treasure, as the name Vogel became associated with unbelievable discoveries about crystals, what they could do, and how you could use them in exciting, new ways. I count myself lucky to have attended several of his workshops back in the eighties.[5]

You can find patterns similar to those written about in this section with Mozart (1756–1791) and Winston Churchill (1874–1965).

MORE CONTEMPORARY ACCOUNTS

Valerie V. Hunt, Ph.D. Dr. Hunt was the very first researcher to objectify electronically the aura of light around people, places, and things. She showed that the aura not only exists but has specific color frequencies that register consistent and measurable waveforms. Her work is a scientific milestone. Her early years were difficult— in a coma at three, almost died, then had a near-death experience. Considered a mystical child by her mother, she was so far ahead of anyone else that kids avoided her. She escaped school pressures by composing poetry, drawing, singing, and thoroughly indulging in the spirit realms around her. Before the coma she had been outgoing, exuberant. Afterward, she became serious, quiet. She says, "One day, quite by surprise, my parents took away my paints, my paper, my crayons, and my books. No one wanted to hear about the fun things my mind created. I mumbled to myself angrily with little satisfaction. My parents didn't listen. Finally, I flashed back to my months in a coma when I experienced being with God in a beautiful land of flowers, sweetness, and love; quiet serenity. I wanted to stay forever, but I recalled that God had said I would go back to the world to bring it beauty. I complained because I did not like the world, and besides I had no talents for beauty. I was just a little girl who sensed beauty but didn't know how to create it. I remember God assuring me that I would be given ample talents to do my 'beauty work.' It was then that I became aware of people, the room, and things I had known before. I had returned from my distant journey." Dr. Hunt expresses a common lament of child near-death experiencers when she says, "Although I had been enthralled at my post-coma skills, there was also a haunting suddenness to my change that was scary, particularly when adults said it was not real." Her full story, including her twenty-five years spent as one of the foremost researchers in the science of human energy fields, is chronicled in her book, *Infinite Mind*.*

Olaf Sunden, Ph.D. Dr. Sunden survived a botched tonsillectomy at age fourteen. At the point when the doctor and his nurse were panicking, he left his body and was suddenly witness to the entire universe and saw that it had no boundaries. There were bubbles, like soap bubbles, in spherical, concentric trains that moved in intricate patterns. He totally understood what he was seeing and what it meant at the time, for he had entered the state of all knowledge. Dr. Melvin Morse, who had met Dr. Sunden and visited with him, was able to fill in more to the story: "He asked that he be permitted to retain the information of molecular

---

Infinite Mind: Science of the Human Vibrations of Consciousness (Malibu, Calif.: Malibu Publishing Co., 1966) Dr. Hunt has also created many music and audio recordings, including a DVD on the human energy field. See "Resources" for more information.

chemistry and quantum interactions on the subatomic level, this 'new physics' as he put it. This was 'granted' or more accurately, occurred, as he didn't seem to be interacting with an agent that granted wishes but rather a fundamental force of the universe. He went on to get his Ph.D. in chemistry of some specialized sort and obtained patents with the understandings that he gained from the basic fundamental insights that he had from his near-death experience, coupled with his specific studies in chemistry. These patents were of a nature that made him money but also helped humanity, for example, how to create paper pulp using less wood products—which of course preserves the raw material of the environment. His story is very striking. He was very clear that he believed that our visions are the starting point of information but have to be followed up with hard work, scientific and scholarly studies, which Olaf felt he achieved and had the scientific patents to back it up."[6] Olaf, by the way, has 100 chemical patents in his name.

Bernie Siegel, M.D. "When I was four years old I was home in bed with one of my frequent ear infections. I took a toy telephone I was playing with and unscrewed the dial and put all the pieces in my mouth, as I had seen carpenters do with nails, which they then pulled out to use. The problem was that I aspirated the pieces and went into laryngo-spasm. I can still feel my intercostal muscles and diaphragm contracting forcefully, trying to get some air into my lungs, but nothing worked and I was unable to make any sounds to attract help. I had no sense of the time but suddenly realized I was not struggling anymore. I was now at the head of the bed watching myself dying. I found it fascinating to be free of my body and a blessing. I never stopped to think about how I could still see and think while out of my body. I was feeling sorry that my mother, who was in the kitchen, would find me dead; but I thought it over and found my new state preferable and intellectually chose death over life. Then the boy on the bed had an agonal seizure, vomited and all the toy pieces came flying out. He began to breathe again, and I was very angry as I returned to my body against my will. I can still remember yelling, 'Who did that?' My thought as a four-year-old was that there was a God who had a schedule and I wasn't supposed to die now. So, an angel apparently did a Heimlich maneuver on him, is the way I would explain it today."

A retired pediatric surgeon, Dr. Siegel is now recognized internationally as an expert in the field of cancer treatment and complementary medicine, always emphasizing the relationship between the patient and the healing process. He has authored numerous books, including the bestseller, *Love, Medicine, and Miracles,** and he is dedicated to helping people heal themselves and live a healthier, more spiritual life.

Benedict Cumberbatch. A popular movie star and theater actor, Cumberbatch cheated death four times: the first from hypothermia when he was a baby, the second when a bomb exploded close by the school he was attending, then again from dehydration and near-starvation while hiking in Tibet during the year after he graduated from high school (known as the "gap year"), and again as a young man when he was abducted, tied up, stuffed into a car, driven to an unknown location, and forced to his knees with a gun muzzle to the head. His captors suddenly just up and fled—no reason given, nothing said.

What is most interesting is the incident as a baby when he nearly froze to death, and how throughout his growing years he was consistently considered "odd." The "freeze affair" occurred because of what his half-sister, Tracy, did. His parents lived in a top-floor flat and would often carry his pram up to the roof whenever he was fussy, pointing him skyward. Tracy did the same thing . . . then forgot him. He was nearly blue when she rushed to the roof. She used the radiator to thaw him out. He grew up remembering "a vision of sky" from his rooftop

---

**Love, Medicine, and Miracles* (Fort Mill, S.C.: Quill, 1990). Dr. Siegel also has his own radio show and is very active, offering videos, articles, and social media interactions. For his website, search on "Bernie Siegel MD."

episodes. But that's not all that set him apart from family, friends, and age-mates. Gregarious in school, Cumberbatch thrived on challenge and seemed filled with plenty of self-confidence even when he made one mistake after another. He believed in himself, his talent, and his intuitive grasp of what lay before him. Unusually intelligent, he matched brains with creativity to excel in painting. He rejected ideas about good and evil, heroes and villains, at an early age. When the gap year came, he went to Tibet and taught English at a Buddhist monastery, adopting the Buddhist philosophy as his own. Always looking for the infinite, the truth behind what seemed true, he learned hard lessons from overdoing—too much partying, booze, and pills—mostly that his body couldn't handle what others could. He was too sensitive. He is quoted as saying: "I don't seek. I don't avoid. I just follow my path, and do my best."

Cumberbatch's keen mind led him early on to being an observer. He continuously feels more, notices more, hears more than most people. He is precise, has problems understanding social media, and is more devoted to social justice and charitable projects than pleasing fans. His hyperaware nature has enabled him to play tormented, brilliant loners in most of his movies, television, and theater roles, as few can. He announced early in 2018 that he would refuse to star in any role unless women actors in that same production were paid as much as the men, including him. He also was hailed as a hero for jumping out of an Uber car ride to race to the aid of a cyclist who was being mugged by four assailants in London.

Akiane Kramarik. An artistic child genius of breathtaking ability, Akiane is best known for the portrait she painted of Jesus when she was eight. Raised by an atheist mother and a disinterested Catholic father, her parents could not afford a television set nor did they have a radio. She had no way to learn about either God or Jesus, plus she was homeschooled. She said her portrait of Jesus was based on a vision she had. When Akiane was a babe, her mother tripped while climbing the disintegrating concrete stairs to their home. Her daughter fell out of her arms and landed face first on hard, crumbling asphalt. Both mother and daughter were in tears. The same day of the accident, her mother received a strange phone call from a woman with a thick Russian accent, telling her that her newborn had an extraordinary future. No one knew who the caller was.

One morning when Akiane was four, she told her mother she had met God. When asked where she learned the word God, she replied "You wouldn't understand." She began drawing soon after. Within weeks, her parents realized she wasn't imagining things. Some days she would describe her visions of heaven where animals talked and plants moved and sang. Eventually, her skeptical parents became believers.

When she was six, her parents displayed her drawings at local arts and crafts fairs. No one would believe such a young child could produce such exquisite illustrations. When she was seven, she began to write poetry. She revealed that the words came to her in prayer. Her first poems were written in a combination of Lithuanian (her mother is Lithuanian) and Russian but eventually she wrote only in English. One day she told her mother that she had been with God again and was told to pray constantly. God, she claimed, told her she needed to rise early in the morning to get ready for her mission. She would not reveal what that mission was; instead, telling her mother, "I hope one day I'll be able to paint what I've been shown."[7]

Akiane is now a teenager. She has written a book titled *Akiane: Her Life, Her Art, Her Poetry* and continues to amaze the world with her ever-expanding abilities and her deep understanding of God and the truth of spiritual realities.*

Ari Hallmark. On December 19, 2011, Todd C. Frankel, staff writer for the *St. Louis Post-Dispatch,* wrote an article titled "The Butterfly

---

*You are urged to get on Akiane's website, named simply, Akiane, and be absolutely wowed at her ever-increasing ability as an artist. There are simply no words to explain her gift and her deep and abiding love of God. You can also find her on YouTube.

People of Joplin." In the article he quoted some of the children who were caught up in the disastrous May 22 Joplin, Missouri, tornado that nearly wiped the thriving city off the map. The children spoke of "butterfly people" in and around the tornado itself. The kids said the butterfly people protected them. Some townsfolk claimed they were guardian angels. Others dismissed the whole thing as a child's fanciful imagination. But those who saw the phenomenon never changed their story; they believed there really were butterfly people flying around and up inside Joplin's terrible tornado, trying to help them. I was called in on this incident by Frankel because of my background in working with child experiencers of near-death states. What impressed me was the number of such sightings and that none of the smaller children ever used the term *angel*. This is significant, as child experiencers never say "angel" unless previously exposed to the term by family or friends. Little ones instead say things like "bright ones" or "the people." The fact that the Joplin kids named the special beings who helped them "butterfly people" made sense.

Ari was part of this tragedy. She was six when the Joplin tornado struck, killing five in her family and leaving her in a field all alone. With help from friends and relatives, she later wrote *To Heaven after the Storm*.[8] Only she and her cousin Julie survived. Ari said she was with her family members in heaven for a while. While there she saw her father, Shane, with hair (he had been bald all her life). He didn't have his glasses, nor were the marks of how he once wore them present. With all the media hype that later occurred, she switched terms and now calls the butterfly people "angels." When I tracked down her book I spoke on the phone with several people who knew her. They confirmed this additional piece to the story Carson Clark, a television news reporter, had televised: *Ari somehow "knew" her parents were going to die about six months before they did. Knowing she could not change what was about to happen, she spent that precious time she had left enjoying them.*[9] A couple of things to note: she knew in advance what was about to happen and once in heaven she noted her father looked better than before. Sometimes children make things up, but this time there were far too many, all with the same story—*the butterfly people were here to help them.* I consider this event important. It shows us the wisdom of listening to children with an open mind. Sometimes they're wiser than adults.

Colton Burpo. Colton was not quite four years old when he nearly died during emergency surgery. After recovering, he began to talk about seeing doctors as they worked on him and about the angels who spoke to him once in the heaven world, as well as his friend, Jesus. Pops, too. Pops, however, was his deceased paternal grandfather, a man he never could have possibly known, nor could he ever have heard his grandfather called by the affectionate nickname of "Pops." Colton was shown older photos of his grandfather. Nope, not the man. It wasn't until his father, Todd Burpo, found younger pictures that the boy exclaimed, "Pops, that's Pops," then nonchalantly noted, "You're younger in heaven." This went on and on, Colton knowing things he could not possibly know, always correct, panicking his mother and father and causing all kinds of problems at church. Yes, church, as Todd Burpo was a Methodist minister, and he couldn't handle his son talking about heaven, nor could he believe anything his son said. That is, until Colton spoke of meeting his older sister, the one who had died in his mother's tummy. How could he know about the miscarriage, much less the sex of the child? Without skipping a beat, Colton went on to say that his mother was pregnant again—something she wasn't quite sure about, yet, indeed she was. What is different in the Burpo incident is that the parents finally accepted as true what their son claimed, which is no small thing considering that Reverend Burpo's position as a minister was in jeopardy until his congregants reconsidered. Todd Burpo, assisted by Lynn Vincent, wrote the book, *Heaven Is for Real,* [10] which became a major motion picture in 2014. It was a smash hit!

Annabel Beam. Producer DeVon Franklin's film *Miracles from Heaven,* opened up to U.S. audiences in 2016 and starred Jennifer Garner as the young girl's mother. The movie focused on a little girl named Annabel Beam who survived a harrowing real-life ordeal back in 2011—she was trapped for hours inside a hollowed-out tree. Franklin specifically addressed Annabel's chronic intestinal pseudo obstruction—a condition her family claims was miraculously healed after she was rescued from inside the tree. Doctors were left with no other explanation for the instant healing except to say the little girl had experienced a "medically spontaneous remission." Franklin and the Beam family believe it was all God's handiwork.

The accident happened when Annabel and her sister climbed up thirty feet and sat on a branch. As that section of the tree began to crack, Annabel crawled into a hole in an effort to relieve weight from the branch, not realizing that the tree was hollowed out inside. It was then that she suddenly tumbled deep inside the tree. "She went head-first and ended up falling 30 feet, landing on the top of her skull," Annabel's mother, Christy Wilson Beam,* said. It took rescue workers hours to get Annabel out of the tree, as her family waited in terror to assess their daughter's condition. She was miraculously unharmed despite falling on her head and being entombed inside for hours.

Something even more bizarre happened the next day. "She turns to me and says, 'You know mommy, I went to heaven when I was in that tree,'" Beam recalled. "All I could say was, 'Really?' And she says, 'Yes, and I sat on Jesus' lap and I wanted to stay, mommy, because there's no pain in heaven.'" Beam said her daughter also told her that Jesus said she would be healed of her stomach ailments. This happened. "She's on zero medications," Beam said, adding that the little girl hadn't been hospitalized since and could now eat whatever she wanted.[11]

---

*Christy Wilson Beam wrote the book, *Miracles from Heaven,* on which the movie is based.

*

You may question why Ari, Colton, and Annabel are in this chapter. They're still kids! Look again. What happened to Ari drew a great deal of media attention, especially as far as the "butterfly people" were concerned. This phenomenon was extraordinary and caused everyone who heard about it to reconsider a child's imagination versus actual facts. Far too many spoke of being saved by such "imagineries" to toss off the validity of this miracle. Colton's and Annabel's stories became motion pictures, both selling well and affecting millions worldwide. I would say that all three of these kids made a huge difference to our "universal psyche." The contemporaries mentioned here, as well as the historical figures, are proof that the phenomenon of near-death addresses more than what's on the "other side" of death's curtain. The next two chapters will show you this . . . and more.

SIXTEEN

Markers

My thinking is both strongly left-brained and strongly right-brained (slightly favoring the left in daily life), so I'm at home with scientists and artists alike.

MICHAEL (CASE 74)

hild experiencers typically see the dead, have conversations with angels, manifest stunning psychic abilities, have future memory, see and hear what is invisible to anyone else, and know things beyond their years. Usually parents, relatives, friends, school teachers, and ministers turn against child experiencers, making fun of them, telling them to shut up, claiming it's just imagination gone wild, and demeaning any notion of seeing and talking with "invisibles" or suddenly "knowing" things. To this day, some churches still brand the phenomenon as "the work of the devil." For that reason, the majority "keep it secret," repressing or tucking away what happened to them, convinced that they are somehow "alien." Unbelievable but true: a number of retirees in this study said nothing to anyone *for seventy to eighty years.* When they were told they could at last say whatever they wanted and it was okay, some cried, others flooded my office with "forbidden" memories.

Learning about near-death experiences and what is typical for children is a must, not only for families but for the kids themselves—no matter how old they are! It is time for society to take "the covers" off this subject. We've done that for adults. Now it's time for the kids.

This chapter opens that door by first giving you a reminder of what to look for, then by offering more specific "markers" to help everyone have a better sense of how child experiencers can change right away and over time. Fraud is tackled after that, and the conundrum of who the real trickster is—the individual who lies about coming back from death with "revelations" or the public at large whose rush to judgment can reveal more about their own prejudices than what might really be true.

THE PATTERN IN GENERAL

Look for:

- *A serious illness or accident that occurs around birth and/or up to five years.* Ask about any problems with the mother's pregnancy, womb issues, or dreams/visions about the situation that might have been remembered or recorded. The same during the toddlerhood, nursery school, and kindergarten years.
- *Marked differences in behavior afterward.* The child may be ahead of or different from age-mates, becoming more so as the years pass, as well as taking on a more nontraditional or nonconformist attitude. He or she may possess a charm or charisma that attracts people, animals, birds, and so on. He or she may appear somewhat backward socially when young while still being unusually creative, clever, and bold. Unafraid of death.
- *A pattern to the aftereffects is present.* Some display electrical sensitivity; most a unique sensitivity to light and sound, and especially pharmaceuticals. Even though the majority go on to exhibit good health, there is a noticeable increase in numerous sensitivities and allergies. School is often a problem, but not for the usual

reasons—most know more than the teacher does. Boredom is an issue.

- *An almost obsessive drive to accomplish a particular task or project, as if it were their mission to do so.* Most will work with no sense of time or money or recognition, yet are inclined to own a home or be aligned with unusual places or ways of living. Marriage interests them but not necessarily a traditional life.

As detailed in the last chapter, children who have experienced near-death events exhibit four main characteristics: a serious illness or accident that occurs around birth and/or up to five years old, marked differences in behavior afterward, a pattern of aftereffects, and an almost obsessive drive to accomplish a particular task or project.

The child's vision of heaven or of any of the other worlds beyond death is alive with a sense of truth and realness that challenges families, teachers, and therapists. Theirs is not just a vision but an experience that both colors their sense of the life they are living and the purpose behind their life. That many repress or tuck away their experience speaks to how they are treated and whether or not they are believed or even allowed to share their story in the first place.

You do not find the high divorce rates and job losses with child experiencers as you do with adult experiencers. Maybe that's because of the added years they have to figure things out and explore possibilities . . . years that they really need to integrate what happened. Seldom, though, are any adults in their life helpful, and that includes therapists who "go by the book."

In my work, I've noticed three main types of child experiencers:

1. *Those who are quiet and more reserved, often aware of a mission and the commitment necessary to fulfill that mission.* They are careful observers, loving, and sensitive—*when they feel safe*—and drawn to creativity and helping others.

2. *Those who seem numb or shell-shocked by their experience and how different they are now from age-mates.* They are more likely to be made fun of or put down by others. They may turn to alcohol or drugs; prone to ignore or repress their memories.

3. *Those who act out or become angry and tend to set themselves apart.* They are restless, and impatient and can be argumentative. May appear confused about differences between "here" and "there." They are visionary knowers and can be pushy and energetic.

Curiously, the vast majority of children rescued from death's finality by advanced technology have near-death experiences that prepare them for, well, advanced technology. Equally curious, children in general born since around 1982, the very year the personal computer made it to the marketplace with the Digital Age right behind, are the very citizens made to order for nanoseconds, NOOKs and Kindles, robotics, and photons. The people our world needs is what our world is producing. My work with near-death kids is what alerted me to the new kids now coming in.

While double-checking research with children who had undergone near-death states, I began to notice ordinary, typical kids, the newest of the new, being born with traits similar to and sometimes the same as the ones I was researching. This isn't possible. I don't care how you look at the phenomenon, or what numbers you crunch, these two very different groups of children cannot be a match or even a near-match . . . but they are! The only thing that could possibly account for this is evolution—the evolution of the human species. We are being prepared as a society, and globally, for another way of living that is untethered to the past. If you don't believe me, just look around you—in your own family and in the news. Today's kids are different—in somewhat similar ways to near-death kids. Spooky, huh? Should you wish to further explore this notion, read my book *Children of the Fifth World*.[1]

MORE SPECIFIC MARKERS

I have published the following list before; it's in several of my books. This time, however, the list is longer and more in-depth, and that's because I've noticed more, dug deeper, and have had numerous occasions to double-check, then double-check again. Society, parents, therapists, and doctors all need to know "the lay of the land" so they can better adjust and manage their role in assisting children who have had near-death experiences, regardless of their present age. I do not intend this list to cover every child or every situation, especially as they age. But I do intend that it offers everyone, experiencers and interested parties alike, a pattern of recognition that I hope will be helpful. Seldom will any one child exhibit all of these markers (although many do). Usually about two-thirds of the characteristics listed is average. To the experiencer I say: relax; we now know how different you are, and it's okay!

MARKERS

Nontraditional, nonconformist attitude
Unique way of thinking, may abstract at young ages
May lose bonding to parents—some or most
May feel foreign in family and with siblings, bond to other side
May go through periods of being "homesick" for the other side
Breathing may stop on occasion, yet mind functions as usual
Charm or charisma, especially with birds, animals, even plants
Socially backward during growing years
Often wake up between 3:00 to 4:00 am
Unafraid of death, bold
Highly intuitive, knowing, creative
Aware of things in the future
Sensing in multiples, synesthesia
Unique sensitivity to light and sound, especially if outside during

brightest time of the day; also need to be careful of pitch/volume of sound at concerts, dances, shows, jams, Bluetooth phone, and music players

Sensitive to touch, taste, texture, and smell

Heightened sensitivity to emotions and environment; empathic

Tend to have allergies

School is a problem; bored easily, very intelligent

Drawn to the spiritual, spirit worlds, prayerful settings

May see ghosts, disincarnates, spirits

Obsessive drive to accomplish tasks and projects

Can be "mission" oriented as years pass

No sense of time/money, yet want a home that is theirs

Prefer open windows, open closets, open doors

Tend to "off angle" placements, designs, furniture

Prefer nontraditional relationships, yet want a marriage that lasts

Display absorption tendencies—the ability to merge

Exhibit dissociation tendencies—the ability to detach

Have a special relationship with electricity, electrical sensitivity; need to be careful of lightning, earthquakes, and tornados (all have unique electrical components) and refrain from living near electrical power stations

Can be hypersensitive to pharmaceuticals and drugs

May search for heaven or missing worlds, even lifelong

Truth and meaning are very important

Can be withdrawn or quiet; keen observers

Could have challenges with depression and suicidal thoughts

Are service-oriented; can be healers

Decidedly independent, inventive, clever

Sense of a higher purpose to life, a God, or a Higher Source of Love

See all things as alive, even rocks

Challenged to understand how society works

I consider all I have just listed to be normal, typical behaviors of children who had a near-death experience. Adult experiencers have some of these traits too. The biggest difference between them: adults take on such characteristics after a disruptive experience in their life; children know no other truth or little else, for this is the world they were birthed from and may still be "attached" to. Comparing the two groups is like comparing apples with oranges. Both are fruits, yet very unique stand-alone types of their own.

A word of caution: there's one very unique trait kids can have *but not adults:* they can harbor a sense of guilt for ever having left HOME or a sense of betrayal, feeling like for whatever reason they were "kicked out." That sense of HOME is more acute with children than adults. Although adults can carry within them a strange "homesickness" and desire to "go back," with children that urge is stronger and uniquely linked to how a child thinks: whenever anything goes wrong, they tend to think "it's their fault" and they should be punished. A lack of self-esteem can linger for decades because of this fear.

Cindy (case 120) reminds us about the "breathing thing" and how strange it can be. "I am particularly interested in the vagus nerve. I have actually experienced this when I used to do handwriting analysis for clients. I was so intent on tuning in, I would stop breathing. Once when someone was observing me, he said, 'Cindy, BREATHE,' and I looked at him and said 'What?' He said I had stopped breathing and I had no idea this occurred. I was breathing but my lungs were not moving."

I am not medically versed enough to understand all the ins and outs of vagus nerve function, but I do know medical science doesn't know as much about the vagus nerve as they think they do. Near-death experiencers, both children and adults, are living proof that the vagus has more functions than we know . . . perhaps among them being the physical counterpoint to the "silver cord"—what mystics say enables our soul to stick with our body.

For fun, just to show you how clever near-death kids can be,

Michael (case 74), whose quote began this chapter, figured out his mother's biorhythms in advance so he'd know when he could and could not argue with her. Can you imagine a little kid being that smart?

Speaking of smart, this business of high intelligence could use a little clarification. IQs over 132, even up to 150–160 and above, are common with child experiencers—more specifically with newborns, babes, and toddlers, even up to and around five years old. The younger the child, the greater the jump. As previously mentioned, from birth to fifteen months is when the actual wiring of the brain is determined and synapse formation increases twentyfold. This activity uses twice the energy of an adult brain. We have also been told that the temporal lobes develop between three and five years old, enabling the young to explore and experiment with possible roles, future patterns, and continuity of environment. All of this highlights that the impact of a near-death experience, hitting at such crucial times in brain/nerve/synapse/lobe development, is, in many cases, *jump-starting higher brain development and the rise of higher intelligence.*

All true; still, I noticed something else. With this new group, those who complained that they missed the big IQ rise did indeed show incredible leaps in intelligence . . . other kinds of intelligence . . . doing other kinds of things . . . all of them equally important. Did you know there are nine types of intelligence? IQ tests only measure one of them. How about the other eight? In all fairness to those who became great in other arenas of life and its living, here are the full nine. Remember, unique abilities within any of these *is a sign of genius.* And this applies double with near-death kids.

THE NINE TYPES OF INTELLIGENCE

1. *Naturalistic.* Drawn to nature, exceptional connections with animals, birds, insects, fish; understands soil, water, various terrains.
2. *Music.* Drawn to music—just listening or may excel at playing instruments; an understanding of scales, tones, vibration, emotional swells.

3. *Logical/mathematical.* A driving need for answers; ability to calculate, reason, and mull over possibilities; abstract thinking.

4. *Existential.* Deep thoughts on the how-tos and whys and wherefores of life and death; explore questions; philosophical.

5. *Interpersonal.* Unique ability to get along with others; good communication skills both verbal and nonverbal; can sense temperaments; open to a myriad of viewpoints.

6. *Bodily-kinesthetic.* Graceful, body smart, with a perfect sense of timing and coordination; dancers and athletes.

7. *Linguistics.* Capacity to think in words and appoint complex meanings; express through language, puzzles, and storytelling.

8. *Intrapersonal.* Understand self (self-smart) and use that understanding to plan life; knows human condition; tends to be shy; psychologists, philosophers, writers.

9. *Spatial.* "Picture" smart; consider beings in three dimensions; image manipulation; dynamic imagination; artists, graphic designers.

Remember these ranges of intelligence types. Just because a child doesn't display the makings of a physicist or surgeon, doesn't mean that child is not brilliant. Many high IQ scores play out in unexpected ways as the child matures. For example: a lot become successful business entrepreneurs, inventors, professional artists and musicians, but just about that many others become farmers who connect with animals and soil in ways that are almost magical, healers of all sorts, and those who help the dying.

If you have a little one right now who could well be an experiencer, allow me to submit a few general tips that may prove helpful:*

---

*There is also a large section in back of *The New Children and Near-Death Experiences* that has numerous suggestions and ideas of how to work with child experiencers of near-death states. Called "Tips for the Child in All of Us," it begins on page 190 and runs through page 232.

Sleep patterns abruptly change afterward. Less nap time, increased flow states, and restlessness. Some may fear sleep and suffer nightmares; others seem exhausted on waking as if they had "toured the universe" or attended "night school" while asleep. Reliving the episode in the dream state is commonplace. Teach simple visualization techniques to use for recall, along with cautions about over use. Life is NOW. Listen.

Love changes for experiencers. It is *normal* for them to lose the parent/child bonding. This doesn't mean they cease to be loving and thoughtful, but it does mean they tend to act more distant than before. The child switches gears and begins to mature faster, becoming more independent. Interests change.

Most kids have a marked decrease in their ability to express themselves and socialize. Since language is *the* most critical skill anyone has, stimulate the child's speech with your own. Promote dialogue with question/answer games, group storytelling, reading out loud, or speaking on pretend microphones. Encourage the child to participate in community projects as a volunteer.

Writing and drawing are just as important as dialogue. Ask the child to make a special book about his or her near-death experience. Have lots of paper handy for pages that cover the newspaper account of the death event (if any), drawings of each aspect of the episode, a description of what happened, information about dreams afterward, sketches of any "beings" that continue to appear, poems, ideas, thoughts, and extra room to record more later on. Have the child choose a title; bind the book with ribbon. A project such as this validates the near-death episode—*as well as the child's feelings.* The parent should keep a journal on the whole affair, too. This helps restimulate parent/child bonding and can serve as an invaluable resource once the child matures. Note: I know I recommended this project a few chapters back, but it's so important I did so again. The parent's journal is just as important!

Child experiencers tend to withdraw and can even reject hugs and cuddles. Recenter them in their bodies through touch: pat their shoulder when you pass by, touch their hand if you speak to them, nudge a knee from time to time, rub their neck. Smile. Teach them to pat and nudge you like you do them. Pets are wonderful for touch therapy, as are plants. Make cookies that the child can help prepare, then turn him or her loose shaping cookies by hand into imaginative designs. Food sculptures are great.

Speaking of food, watch sugar levels. Child experiencers are more sensitive than the average child to chemicals, excessive sweets, refined sugars, and chemical replacements. Practice good nutrition; use veggies and fruit for snacks. Full-spectrum lights are preferred to florescent; avoid overexposure to electrical items (especially electric blankets) and power lines. Cotton usually works best for clothes and bedding. At meals have a burning candle for a centerpiece (or flowers) and say the type of grace where each person in turn can offer his or her own prayer.

Ideally, child experiencers and adult experiencers should get together once in a while, for each can support the other. Adults can provide that special atmosphere for "talking about it" amongst experiencers and socializing within a peer group. It's the kids, though, that can inspire confidence and stability, as kids are much more understanding and open than their elders. Above all, parents who were experiencers when young should be encouraged to speak of their own experience and what they went through afterward *in front of their child experiencer!* Most don't. Such a sharing has a positive ripple effect for years to come!

FRAUD/BACKLASH

I was quite startled by a phone call I received after *The New Children and Near-Death Experiences* was published. A young woman said her mother "stole" what happened to her as a child and used it, lied to others, lied to me, saying this was what she had gone through and she wanted to share her story to help others. What? The daughter would not give me names, hers or her mother's. She phoned to just let me

know her mother lied. Then she hung up as if ashamed—of her mother
or of herself for letting her mother get away with the ruse? Before she
hung up, she offered that her mother did it for attention . . . as if that
made it right.

What a surprise!

To this day I do not know who this mother/daughter duo is. Nearly
half of the people in that study I either spoke to personally or on the
phone or visited with them and their family. The rest were contacted
by mail or email several times. As I recall, their stories checked. We're
talking about 277 people. Apparently one slipped through the verifying
I try to do. Has that happened to me before? Yes, but almost entirely
with adults. Some adult experiencers are really too anxious to be on
television, write a book, or be a media star (although they deny that).
But it's obvious.

Usually you can tell if someone is lying to you about his or her experience. There's a certain look in their eyes when they're speaking to you,
or something odd about the way shoulders and legs bend as if leaving
would be a better option. And, sometimes it's about the way people talk
. . . as if the tone of their voice is somehow forced or pushed or too
good/too great/too polished. I watch hips, too, as a way to "measure"
their comfort zone. If you don't understand body language, I suggest
you take some classes. I learned from watching my police officer father
"read" people. When interviewing kids, their parents or familiar elders
(school teachers, aunts and uncles, and so on) *cannot be present.* Won't
work if they are, as the child will always try to please familiar elders
rather than taking the risk that maybe they can say whatever they wish
"to a stranger." Body language makes a huge difference with little ones.
You never, never, have your eyes above theirs. That puts you in the position of "authority" when what you want is to create moments of simple
friendship and sharing.

The issue of fraud/backlash involves far more than if some "pretend" experiencer is trying to "pull the wool over your eyes." Often

it involves deeper issues, like the reputation of a family or how they might appear to others or be judged by the God they believe in. One case like this that garnered a great deal of national attention involved Alex Malarkey, who in 2004 and at the age of six was paralyzed and in a comma for two months following a horrific car accident. When he regained consciousness, he was effusive about seeing Jesus, angels, and heaven itself. All of this appeared very legit considering what had happened to him. His father was so excited and touched by his son's story that he wrote *The Boy Who Came Back from Heaven*,[2] a book that became a bestseller. Alex's story and his father's book opened up the fabled Pandora's box in the sense of how his mother, from the start, kept saying Alex's vision was not in accord with "what's in the Bible." Yes, they were fundamental Christians with a strict idea of whos and whats. There were continual arguments, religious backlashes, claims and counterclaims, with a demand later on that the book's publication cease. Parents divorced. Alex stayed with his mother. Once he reached the age of consent, via a nationwide media interview, Alex denied his story, saying he made the whole thing up for the attention he would receive—he said he lied.

End of story? Maybe.

Last I heard there was a lawsuit ongoing in the Malarkey family as to where all that money from book sales went. This issue erupted around the same basic time frame as the media frenzy surrounding the Colton Burpo story/book/movie, followed by Annabel Beam's story/book/movie. Three in a row. Later, Colton's minister father was threatened numerous times by the faith elders of his church as to whether or not he could continue as their minister. Annabel Beam's case is still stirring up backlash as to its accuracy. The larger Christian publishers in our nation were told by powerful church leaders to cease publication of anything that talked about heaven, that all the heaven anyone needed to know about was in the Bible.

End of story? I don't think so.

There is reason to wonder if the continual pressure put on Alex by his mother is what may have caused him to change his mind. There is reason to wonder about the "faith" of those in Burpo's church and within his church's hierarchy . . . could they handle a real miracle or was that somehow "a stretch too far?" Why was Annabel Beam criticized as harshly as she was, when there was ample proof at the accident scene, at the hospital, and in how she was cured of a serious medical condition virtually overnight? If not proof enough, if not truly modern miracles, then how do we handle backlash? It is right for anyone to question what seems impossible, as fraud does occur. But, in these specific cases, the children and their families deserved far more public fairness and grace than they received.

End of story? Not hardly.

There is a case ping-ponging all over the Internet of a Buddhist monk who was told during his near-death experience, "If you don't believe in Jesus Christ, you are going to hell." Yes, he is an adult experiencer and, yes, he is now evangelizing that "Buddhism is fake, and everyone must become Christians," which is endorsed by happy Christians in support of what he was told. Don't think for one moment that something this vile only happens with adults taking on adults. A few years ago, when I was a speaker at a near-death conference held in San Antonio, Texas, a mother and her young son requested time with me. What they shared was unbelievable. The boy had nearly died during complex brain surgery, had a vivid near-death experience, and felt led to share his story afterward—about angels, heaven worlds, and God's eternal love. A contingent of elders from their church began visiting them *every week afterward and still were—I'm talking months here,* condemning the boy for "making up" everything he claimed to have seen and for telling folks about it. He and his family were now considered pariahs and were faced with having to move away to find peace.

Not to pick on Christians here, I've run across children from Muslim faiths in Egypt and in Turkey who were condemned to death *by their parents,* for embarrassing the family by telling lies that demeaned their faith and their family's honor. One of these children was two years old when her near-death experience occurred. Her own mother damned her the loudest. The other two were a few years older. Same "crime" according to parents (talking about heaven and the God of All People); same solution: death. All three survived through the kindness of strangers and finally, when older, emigrated to different cities in Europe.

Did you know that complicated children's near-death scenarios occur often in other countries of the world? Especially in Asian cultures, children are judged for their behavior and are told how they must live to become good adults. In various African cultures, hellish experiences are fairly common with children, rather than with adults. You cannot use anyone's case anywhere on this planet as a singular "guide from on high" or as proof of good or bad behavior. Never was it "I'm right, you're wrong." Thanks to social media and the Internet, near-death stories are gaining prominence, while good research fades. *And those stories have become "demandments" of what is true and what is fiction and what we should believe or not believe.* Never was it meant to be this way, and that concerns me.

What we are losing here with accounts of near-death experiences, even near-death-like experiences, is *the edge of things where subtlety reigns.* That's where people like me come in; people who can say there's more to the story. None of this ends where you think it might. Actually, it doesn't end at all.

SEVENTEEN

The Forever Angels

I call it a near-birth experience. Yes, my body, but my spirit and soul are birthed into another dimension.

JAMES (CASE 99)

*O*ne day, while walking along the back roads north of Roanoke, Virginia, where the pavement ended, I happened upon a small cemetery and there I saw, plain as you please, a young boy waiting near a gravestone. It seemed very strange to me that he was alone. Too young for that, I thought. I walked up to him and asked what he was doing there. He replied, "I'm waiting for my parents." A curious answer, plus, it was late afternoon. So I asked again, hoping he would say more, and he did. "My parents said I could not leave without their permission, so I have to wait here until they come back." I looked at the gravestone. Chiseled across were words noting the recent death of a young boy about the age and probably the same size of the one I was talking to. On a hunch, I asked, "Did you die?" He said yes, but he couldn't go anywhere until his parents gave him permission to do so. With that, I finally realized I was talking to the boy's ghost, his soul. There was no hint of this. No mental telepathy involved. He was as real as any boy could be, his voice full of childhood. I immediately switched to "mother mode" and assured him it was okay with his parents if he went on into the bright worlds that called him. He would still be able to check in with them once in a while—maybe through dreams or whispers. Hardly five minutes passed. He smiled, started to turn, then vanished.

This is how real it is . . . for the child newly dead who has yet to cross over and the child who crossed over but rushed right back.

Near-death experiences take us places few other experiences can. Newbies, once verbal, speak of things our society has deemed secret or made up. Endlessly fascinating, terrifying, wondrous, and challenging, their voices both bless and sting like that of the boy I found standing next to his own gravestone. There was nothing about him to suggest he might be a ghost. The situation he was in became a forever reminder to me that, until we can embrace the "in-between" of life's edges, we cannot hope to know the real truth behind what seems true.

This book is my attempt to do that, to go where other researchers have not, and to look with eyes that register subtlety as carefully as evidence. Both are equally important. Since 1978, I've had the privilege of touching the lives of nearly 5,000 adult and child experiencers, and they have touched mine. Always I asked, "What was it like for you?"

Scientific protocols are wonderful. They set the bar for how society can consider truth. Missed entirely, though, is the flesh and blood of those who wonder and the tears of those who cry. We must be open to every bit of evidence, every stroke of movement, every thought/feeling/ heartbeat of those who came back; who brought with them stories they never could have fabricated—at least not convincingly.

Look at it this way: *Vertical questions establish facts,* what can be proved or at least stand up to verification, so we can have structure to build on. *Horizontal questions open the doors of emotion and feeling and memories beyond words,* how we live and where we go in our mind. We lead by our questions. We need both styles to mirror back to us who we are. Child experiencers don't have mirrors for comparisons. They have only memories. I believe this is the main reason why they are easily lost within the family and the social groups around them.

I call this book *The Forever Angels* because it is an in-depth look at tiny ones who are forever part of where they left. If you count both of the studies I have done with child experiencers of near-death states, the total is 397 . . . angels all. These two studies show us that no matter how long child experiencers live, the vast majority never lose their sense of HOME, the memory of where they came from, where we all came from. They still remember. We forgot.

Birthers are still part of where they left. What I've noticed is that once they leave the womb, certainly realities switch. But with this switch, they seem to cling more to the imaginal realms, perhaps in an effort to hold on to that "perfect" world where they once were. Family and social groups brand whatever seems odd in a child's behavior as overimaginative or false, not realizing there is a huge difference between what is made up (imagined) and what is preexistent (imaginal). We abandon the soul of our children when we think that training their minds is our only job. We tend to close doors before we realize that a door was ever there to begin with.

Adult experiencers recognize differences (before and after) and tend to clear out or alter whatever once existed to make room for "the new," adjusting as necessary. Child experiencers, depending on age, are unaware of differences at first. The switching around they face never made sense to them. Extremes can result . . . to shut out this world as they return to the OTHER. Where adults eventually integrate what happened to them and make it part of their life, *children do just the opposite.* The typical child does not integrate, even decades later, even if busy with life obligations. Instead, they adjust, adapt, compromise, compensate—again and again. For the majority, integration does not occur until the later years of life. Don't confuse "play acting" with maturity. To integrate, child experiencers need the "mirror" mentors can provide to help them openly verbalize and more truly see the self they have become, and hopefully why.

It is true that near-death experiences can emerge from cases of rape, sexual abuse, beatings, or other types of abuse. The most common component reported from any of these is the same as from the phenomenon: out-of-body experiences. When a child is being traumatized or abused, they commonly leave their body and go above, like rising to the ceiling, or hunching up in a ceiling corner. They view the whole episode from that spot . . . a place apart that is safe. In that safe place, kids tend to think with a mature mind, know what is happening, and often why. They stay there until it is safe for them to return to their body. This often happens if abuse becomes an issue. Whether or not these out-of-body experiences are really near-death experiences depends on the pattern of aftereffects. Recheck chapter 16, "Markers." The factor that determines this is intensity. If that out-of-body experience was intense enough, markers will show up. Doesn't matter how many episodes occur. What matters is intensity. Otherwise, atypical patterns just won't be there.

You run into the same issue with a coma—not that it's an abuse issue—but because of what we now know. Many of those who wake up from a coma talk about out-of-body experiences and the ability to still see, hear, think, and move around even when the brain is supposedly shut down. This also applies to blows to the head, high fever, and sometimes drug issues. If few if any markers show up, then the phenomenon is not present. Where this can become almost beyond belief is when kids see and hear things they shouldn't while they are out of their body. I'm thinking here of babes in cribs kept in their parent's bedroom. I've encountered any number of cases where the baby was slapped around to stop the child from crying, breathing stopped, then the babe rose up to witness the goings-on. Fathers are usually the first to scream, "No way! That kid couldn't know or remember anything!" The biggest shock here is that the "baby witness" often could recall the incident years, even decades later—accurately—much to the parent's horror.

A child experiencer goes through a "brain shift." Yup, we can actually say that. I identify a brain shift in what I have seen with children as when the pineal gland jumps ahead of itself; *temporal lobe expansion appears to occur before temporal lobe development; synesthesia or multi-sensory awareness become almost "normal";* the shaking together or clustering of information is noticed;† parallel processing of simultaneous brain waves is occasionally present;‡ moving physical objects with brainwave emissions and a steady focus of thought "just happens."§*

We already know scientifically that *any* experience that overwhelms a person to the degree that thought processes are altered, changes brain structure to some extent. Near-death states and other transformative episodes are capable of producing the same response, which leads in many cases to permanent body-mind changes, accompanied by the awakening of higher levels of consciousness and a curiosity that just doesn't quit.

This can and often does produce "brain growth spurts" where brain

---

*Refer to Richard E. Cytowic, M.D. *The Man Who Tasted Shapes: A Bizarre Medical Mystery Offers Revolutionary Insights into Emotions, Reasoning, and Consciousness.* New York: Tarcher/Putnam, 1993.

†Howard Gardner. *Creating Minds.* New York: Basic Books, 1993. Howard Gardner, a psychologist and codirector of the Harvard Project on Human Potential, profiled great minds of the twentieth century in an attempt to characterize genius. He discovered that discarding accepted ideas of what is possible can make it easier to take new ideas seriously; that connecting the unconnected leads to insight; and that a tolerance for ambiguity is crucial to creativity. He points out that the word *intelligence* means to "select among," indicating the importance of detail recognition. But genius shakes together or clusters information, much as a child would, to arrive at different or larger concepts.

‡Refer to Anna Wise. *High Performance Mind.* New York: Putnam, 1995. Much work has been done since then, continuing the use of Mind Mirror measurements. Mind Mirror is a step up from electroencephalography (EEG) measurements of electrical brain activity. Not only will it read out as an EEG does, but it will split the readout, giving both halves of the brain (left and right) separate billing at the same time. Today, the world's expert with the Mind Mirror is Judith Pennington. An earlier book of hers is *Your Psychic Soul: Embracing Your Sixth Sense* (Virginia Beach, Va.: 4th Dimension Press, 2012). For more information on Judith see "Resources."

§Refer to the original article, "Brain Waves Move Computer Cursors," *New York Times,* March 7, 1995. Such test results are becoming mainstream now. The first I heard of this was with the results from scientists working at the New York State Department of Health in Albany. They were able to teach people *that using thought alone, one could move a computer cursor around a display screen to communicate better.*

cell branches suddenly increase in number and spread rapidly, expanding contact between cells. Scientists suspect that any rise in intelligence has more to do with these spurts than anything else.

Take this seriously: *Growth spurts literally rewire and reconfigure the brain,* making more complex, efficient neural pathways for transmitting information. From this factor—everything else proceeds. And that includes the puzzle of things future.

I first began tracking anomalous events in the midsixties—things like past-life recall, alien sightings, alien abductions, flying dreams, out-of-body episodes, spirit visitations, invisible beings, and other paranormal and psychic occurrences. I found an extraordinary relationship with things future throughout all of these incidents. At any age, but especially between the ages of three and five, there is no natural sense of time or space. Little ones and the very young project into the future intuitively—engaging with futuristic ideas, images, feelings, and sensations. The future does not appear as the future to the very young. To them, the future is simply another aspect of "now" (the immediate), and it remains that way until they are able to establish the validity of what seems continuous and connected. Once they accomplish this, they have the dependable sense they need to adapt to ever-changing environments—like growing up.

The imaginal adventures of childhood are necessary for the development of healthy minds. That's normal. But near-death states that happen during this juncture in brain development appear to accelerate mental growth years ahead of anything expected.

Many even begin to "live" the future ahead of time and remember having done so when the futuristic event actually occurs. I named this "future memory"* because the term fits. Forget déjà vu (which is past oriented). Kids and adults who experience future memory say *it feels more like a rehearsal*—an advanced awareness of the power they have to change

---

*Refer to my book *Future Memory.*

things, to handle stress better, and to become more grounded in their life. But, hold on here.

Research published on the Neuroscience News website blares the headline, "Blue Brain Team Discovers a Multi-Dimensional Universe in Brain Networks."[1] What a team of neuroscientists uncovered is a universe of multidimensional geometric structures and spaces within brain networks *that enables the brain to function in seven, even eleven dimensions. The brain is NOT three-dimensional.* It is many-dimensional, capable of visiting and working within worlds within worlds within worlds—*as a normal aspect of daily use.*

If you think this is amazing, consider the spiritual shift little kids go through. Yes, I said spiritual shift—kids!

Examples: most alien/fairy/monster sightings occur between the ages of three and five; spirituality enters as present and powerful in children's lives at age three; most Catholic saints had a near-death experience when very young; many miracles verified by the Catholic church involved small children; brain shifts with kids appear to "jump-start" the engine of evolution—as spirit shifts advance attitudes and behaviors of the young toward social justice, moral integrity, compassion, and caring.

Do all near-death kids fit this pattern? No. But the majority do. Do all near-death kids love God, see angels, and become religious? Most decidedly not.

Oops.

Puzzle: Children's cases throughout Asia and Africa are often negative or fearful or demand that certain behaviors are honored growing up. . . *yet cases in these same areas that involve birthers, babies, and toddlers seldom ever involve such extremes.* Children's cases throughout the Western world are often uplifting or encouraging, even inspiring . . . *yet if you go after reports from the youngest of the young in those same areas, you encounter more of an "observer" intellect that sees both sides, all sides, positive/negative.*

However you look at it, the consciousness of the very young does not fit anyone's religious categories or beliefs of what is true and what isn't, what is human and what lies beyond what is human.

Fact: the youngest of the young, no matter where they are in the world, know "God," not necessarily by that term, but rather in the sense of All That Is. A surprising number of non-Christian kids know the name Jesus and who he is. They know the tenets of good and evil, right and wrong. But "religion" itself confuses them; any religion, even the idea of religion. To little ones, everything is all about LOVE, not some God/Allah/Deity. Any presence of "God" (most are met by some fatherly or grandfatherly type) if questioned, "Is that what you really look like?" instantly morphs into a brilliance beyond description, a light so powerful it engulfs the world and creation itself, a loving presence beyond definition. That kind of God/Allah/Deity is what newborns wiggle to, babes and toddlers laugh with—a loving presence that permeates and enlivens all that exists, including them, and breathes the world into existence, again and again.

The amazing thing here is even children raised in an atheist family know the presence of God and what God feels like. Children raised according to voodoo rituals *know Jesus by name.* Buddhist and Muslim children nod and grin. And here's something else: child experiencers make a beeline for church whenever they can; yet adult experiencers walk out the door, preferring a more open approach to a more spiritual view of things. Opposites. Do the kids stay in the church they run to? Seldom ever. The God of Love just doesn't seem to be there. Adults, however, eventually come back to some kind of church, preferably a spiritual/metaphysical one.

*

This book is a departure in near-death research. The insistence here has been to examine the phenomenon from every possible angle, to let the very youngest speak—no matter their present age—and compare that with my previous study done in the nineties. It's adults that split differences. Kids don't. They get right to the point, even if we don't believe them.

This has been a three-year project. I've been just as surprised as you for what has tumbled from the lips of those quiet for far too long. Previous research has been done with child experiencers, and you'd think that would have met "the need to know." It didn't.

Why?

Because we thought we knew all about the near-death experience. Thousands of stories have been carefully studied; work is now global. We've really done a pretty good job. Yet tiny ones, some now in their 70s and 80s, still miss HOME. That special homesickness never went away. And most of them *still* wonder what all the fuss has been about concerning life after death. True, some still quiver about that one, yet the vast majority view the whole near-death phenomenon quite differently than we think they do.

I got a real taste of that "difference" during previous conferences of the International Association for Near-Death Studies.* The youngest of the young, especially birthers, have always felt a little lost at these conferences. All the rest of us regard everyone as equals. Adult experiencers, child experiencers . . . any difference must be negligible, right? Wrong!

These folks have consistently felt lost because they could not, and still can't, relate to all the stories told by older kids and adults about unconditional love and joy and learning how to pass them on. How can they converse with their supposed peers when they do not recognize the language adult experiencers use? To an experiencer who knows *only life,* no matter the form or time frame, the challenge is to understand those who focus on a single event as if it were that important. To them, it isn't. Truth for them lies in a much larger story . . . not about death, but about life.

To those who experience near-death as a birther, baby, toddler, or

---

*Anyone can peruse, visit, or join this nonprofit association. For more information see the section "International Association for Near-Death Studies" at the end of this book.

very young child, *the story is about the life continuum, NOT life after death.*

Hear this: Everyone is so enamored about "out-of-the-mouth-of-babes" stories. After all, the innocent know "the real truth." But who pays attention to those kids who amazed us after we leave? Who does follow-ups? Who talks to their families and siblings years later? Yes, previous "afterward" studies about child experiencers have been done . . . what it was like for them growing up. None were truly in-depth. We never took the next step we owed them. Not really. We walked away once we satisfied our hunger for details—about death, what it was like to survive death, and what happened on the other side.

I submit to you that all of us, those who call ourselves researchers and those of the interested public, missed it. We missed learning that the near-death experience casts tremendous light on the life *continuum,* on the notion that there is *always* life. *Never* was it life after death. We've been kidding ourselves about that. *The true subject has always been continuous life.* Children tell us we have always lived, that eternity is our home.

Look again at the stories in this book . . . of those who clearly remember being in the womb and getting "high" every time their mother smoked and feeling terrified every time their mother tried to kill herself, or them. Look at those who remember previous lives, alien lives, endless life. There's simply too many voices to ignore. Worldwide.

As *James (case 99)* said at the beginning of this chapter . . . we are all having a "near-birth experience," moving from one dimension to another in a continuous and forever opportunity to be the angels we really are, have always been, and will always be.

All of us . . . forever angels!

Notes

CHILD EXPERIENCERS ARE DIFFERENT

1. Pim van Lommel, M.D., *Consciousness Beyond Life: The Science of the Near-Death Experience* (New York: HarperOne, 2010); Sam Parnia, M.D., *What Happens When We Die: A Groundbreaking Study into the Nature of Life and Death* (Carlsbad, Calif.: Hay House, 2006); Sam Parnia, M.D., *Erasing Death: The Science That Is Rewriting the Boundaries between Life and Death* (New York: HarperOne, 2013).
2. *I Died Three Times in 1977—The Complete Story* is still available through Amazon. The second book is *Future Memory* (Charlottesville, Va.: Hampton Roads, 1999). The third book is *A Manual for Developing Humans* (Faber, Va.: Rainbow Ridge Books, 2017).
3. To learn more about my work and how I found as many experiencers as I did, read *Near-Death Experiences: The Rest of the Story* (Charlottesville, Va.: Hampton Roads, 2011).
4. Dr. Penny Sartori, *The Wisdom of Near-Death Experiences* (London: Watkins Publishing, 2014).

ONE. WHAT'S HERE

1. Raymond A. Moody, Jr., *Life after Life* (Covington, Ga.: Mockingbird Books, 1975).

FOUR. BIRTH MEMORIES

1. This is part of Marcella's story in Cherie Sutherland's book *Children of the Light: The Near-Death Experiences of Children* (Australia and New Zealand: Bantam Books, 1995), 82–86.

2. David Chamberlain, "Reliability of Birth Memories: Evidence from Mother and Child Pairs in Hypnosis," *Journal of the American Academy of Medical Hypnoanalysis* 1, no. 2 (1996): 89–98. A treasure trove of published clinical studies on birth memory can be obtained through Chamberlain Communications (see "Resources" for more information).

3. David Chamberlain, Ph.D., *The Mind of Your Newborn Baby* (Berkeley, Calif.: North Atlantic Books, 1998). Should you have any difficulty finding this book, call 1-800-733-3000 or visit the North Atlantic Books website.

FIVE. THE WOMB

1. There are numerous references now to fetus/preborn development in the womb, including: Chamberlain, *The Mind of Your Newborn Baby;* Sir William Liley, "The Personality of the Fetus," *Australian and New Zealand Journal of Psychiatry* 6, no. 2 (1972); David Chamberlain, "Babies Are Not What We Thought: Call for a New Paradigm," *International Journal of Prenatal Studies,* (Autumn, 1992); David Chamberlain, "Prenatal Body Language: A New Perspective on Ourselves," *Primal Renaissance: The Journal of Primal Psychology* 14, no. 1/2 (August 1999); Thomas Verny and John Kelly, *The Secret Life of the Unborn Child: How You Can Prepare Yourself for a Happy Healthy Life* (New York: Dell, 1982).

2. Jaap van der Wal, "The Embryo in Us: A Phenomenological Search for Soul and Consciousness in the Prenatal Body," *Birth Psychology* 27, no. 3 (January 2013): 151.

3. See the works of David Chamberlain.

SIX. OTHERWORLDLY

1. Kenneth Ring, Ph.D. and Sharon Cooper, *Mindsight: Near-Death and Out-of-Body Experiences in the Blind* (Palo Alto, Calif.: William James Center for Consciousness Studies, 1999).

2. Titus Rivas, M.A., MSc, Elizabeth M. Carman, L.H.D., Neil J. Carman, Ph.D., and Anny Dirven, "Paranormal Aspects of Pre-Existence Memories in Young Children," *Journal of Near-Death Studies* 34, no. 2 (Winter 2015): 87. Excerpt comes via permission of Janice Holden, editor of the *Journal of Near-Death Studies.* Copies of the article can be obtained from the International Association for Near-Death Studies

(see "International Association for Near-Death Studies" at the end of the book).

3. Sandy Briggs. *Merging with Socrates and Prebirth Memories.* Self-published by author, 2015, ISBN 978-1-4951-6411-8.

4. This discussion between Cebes, Simmias, and Socrates is recorded in "The Phaedo" in *Plato: The Last Days of Socrates.* A good translation of this book is the one by Hugh Tredennick and Harold Tarrant (London: Penguin Books Ltd., 1993), page 135, section 77c and page 135, section 77d.

5. Jim B. Tucker, M.D., *Return to Life: Extraordinary Cases of Children Who Remember Past Lives* (New York: St. Martin's Press, 2015).

SEVEN. SOME SURPRISES

1. Sarah Knapton, "Bright Flash of Light Marks Incredible Moment Life Begins When Sperm Meets Egg," Telegraph website, 4/26/16.

2. Dr. Penny Sartori, *The Wisdom of Near-Death Experiences* (London: Watkins Publishing, 2014).

3. Cherie Sutherland, *Children of the Light.*

4. Kenneth Ring, Ph.D., "Amazing Grace: The Near-Death Experience as a Compensatory Gift," *Journal of Near-Death Studies* 10, no. 1 (Autumn, 1991).

5. For an in-depth discussion on these findings plus actual case studies see P. M. H. Atwater, "Alien Existences," chap. 9 in *The New Children and Near-Death Experiences* (Rochester, Vt.: Bear & Co., 2003). For verification of the importance of the dates see William Strauss and Neil Howe, "Completing the Eras of the Millennial Cycle," in *Generations: The History of America's Future, 1584 to 2069* (New York: Quill/William Morrow, 1991), 377–383.

6. For a startling case of alien abduction at the same moment of a near-death experience, refer to P. M. H. Atwater, "Anomalies" in *Beyond the Light: Startling New Evidence of Life after Death—From Visions of Heaven to Glimpses of Hell* (New York: Avon Books, 1994).

EIGHT. AFTERWARD

1. Judith Orloff, M.D., *The Empath's Survival Guide: Life Strategies for Sensitive People* (New York: Sounds True, 2017).

2. Atwater, *Future Memory.*

NINE. A QUESTION OF FAMILY

1. A drawing of this event can be found in Atwater, *New Children and Near-Death Experiences,* 143.

TEN. HEALTH ISSUES

1. Regarding electrical sensitivity, please refer to the following: *Electrical Phenomena with Weather Extremes,* a newsletter put out by P. M. H. Atwater, L.H.D., July 2014, available on P. M. H. Atwater's website, in the Newsletter section (use the Archive button to search for this edition). Also, search out July 2014 edition of the GalileOProject, Newsletter #31, 7/8/2016, article "Convenience and Communication without Radiation." Also see the following published papers: Sarah Blalock, Med, Janice Minor Holden, Ed.D., and P. M. H. Atwater, L.H.D, "Electromagnetic and Other Environmental Effects Following Near-Death Experiences: A Primer" and Bruce Greyson, M.D., Mitchell B. Liester, M.D., Lee Kinsey, Ph.D., Steven Alsum, M.Div., and Glen Fox, Ph.D., "Electromagnetic Phenomena Reported by Near-Death Experiencers." Both papers appear in *Journal of Near-Death Studies* 33, no. 4 (Summer, 2015).

2. Two excellent sources on homeopathy, both written by doctors: Jennifer Jacobs and Wayne B. Jones, *Healing with Homeopathy: The Complete Guide* (New York: Grand Central Publishing, 1998); Vinton McCabe, *Practical Homeopathy: A Comprehensive Guide to Homeopathic Remedies and Their Acute Uses* (New York: St. Martin's Press, 2000). You might also consider switching your family physician to a Doctor of Osteopathy (D.O.) instead of an M.D. (similar knowledge base, except a D.O. is well-schooled in prevention measures).

THIRTEEN. PTSD AND NDEs

1. Bruce Greyson, "An Overview of Near-Death Experiences," in John C. Hagan, III, ed., *The Science of Near-Death Experiences* (Columbia, Mo.: University of Missouri Press, 2017), 26.

2. Hal Taylor, "Emerging from PTSD," *Venture Inward* (a publication of the Association for Research and Enlightenment [A.R.E.]), (April/

June 2015): 20–22. (See "Resources" for A.R.E.'s contact information.)

3. Pete Walker, *Complex PTSD: From Surviving to Thriving; A Guide and Map for Recovering from Childhood Trauma* (Des Moines, Ia.: Meredith Corporation/Create Space Independent Publishing Platform, 2013).

4. Satwant K. Pasricha, *Making Sense of Near-Death Experiences: A Handbook for Clinicians*, edited by Mahendra Perera, Karuppiah Jagadheesan, and Anthony Peake (London: Jessica Kingsley Publishers, 2012), 100.

5. Bruce H. Lipton and Steve Bhaerman, *Spontaneous Evolution: Our Positive Future (and a Way to Get There from Here)* (Macon, Ga.: Hay House, 2011).

6. Andrew Newberg, M.D., and Mark Robert Waldman, *How God Changes Your Brain: Breakthrough Findings from a Leading Neuroscientist* (New York: Ballantine Books, 2010).

FOURTEEN. SOLUTIONS

1. Dr. Vasquez, personal communication to the author.

FIFTEEN. HISTORICAL CASES

1. Ronald Clark, *Einstein: The Life and Times* (New York: Avon, 1971), 303 quoted in J. "Joe" Timothy Green, Ph.D., "Did Near-Death Experiences Play a Seminal Role in the Formulation of Einstein's Theory of Relativity?" *Journal of Near-Death Studies* 20, no. 1 (Fall 2001): 64–66.

2. John Neihardt, *Black Elk Speaks* (New York: Pocket Books, 1972).

3. Glenn Clark, The Man Who Tapped the Secrets of the Universe (Kessinger Publishing, 2006; first published 1943), 11.

4. P. M. H. Atwater, *The New Children and Near-Death Experiences* (Rochester, Vt.: Bear & Company, 2003), 129.

5. Information covered is paraphrased from the Legacy of Marcel Vogel website and from personal communications with Vogel during his later years. Additional details from his classes have also been incorporated. His thesis is published under Marcel Vogel and Peter Prigsheim, *The Luminescence of Liquids and Solids and Its Practical Application* (Hoboken, N.J.: Wiley Interscience, 1943).

6. Dr. Melvin Morse and I further discussed the case of Olaf Sunden via email dated January 8, 2017.

7. Much of my material about Akiane Kramarik comes from the article by Gary Noel, "Artistic Child Genius," *Today's Astrologer* 78, no. 10. Also see Akiane Kramarik, *Akiane: Her Life, Her Art, Her Poetry* (Nashville, Tenn.: Thomas Nelson, 2006).

8. Ari Hallmark, with Lisa Reburn, Ph.D., *To Heaven after the Storm* (Franklin, Ill.: Truth Book Publishers, 2012).

9. Todd C. Frankel, "The Butterfly People of Joplin," *St. Louis Post-Dispatch* (December 19, 2011); Carson Clark, WHNT News 19, Huntsville, Al., televised news story, "Child Writes Book about Going to Heaven & Surviving a Tornado" (5/15/12). To all these people, thank you for allowing me to make notes of our interaction, and thank you to Ari for being the wise and wonderful young woman you have turned out to be.

10. Todd Burpo and Lynn Vincent, *Heaven Is for Real: A Little Boy's Astounding Story of His Trip to Heaven* (Nashville, Tenn.: Thomas Nelson, 2010).

11. Christy Wilson Beam, *Miracles from Heaven: A Little Girl, Her Journey to Heaven, and Her Amazing Story of Healing* (New York: Hachette Books, 2015).

SIXTEEN. MARKERS

1. P. M. H. Atwater, *Children of the Fifth World: A Guide to the Coming Changes in Human Consciousness* (Rochester, Vt.: Bear & Co., 2012).

2. Kevin Malarkey, *The Boy Who Came Back from Heaven* (Carol Stream, Ill.: Tyndal House, 2010).

SEVENTEEN. THE FOREVER ANGELS

1. "Blue Brain Team Discovers a Multi-Dimensional Universe in Brain Networks," June 12, 2017, on the Neuroscience News website.

Additional and Suggested Reading

BOOKS BY CHILD EXPERIENCERS IN THIS STUDY

Listed below are books that were submitted by child experiencers in this study.

Briggs, Sandy. *A God Experience in the Light: A Transcendent Experience of the Spirit*. Self-published. ISBN 978-1-4951-5181-1; *Merging with Socrates and Prebirth Memories: Spiritually Transformative Experiences*. Self-published. ISBN 978-1-451-6411-8. To inquire about these books, contact Sandy at briggsfmly@windstream.net.

Cull, Linda. *Where the Light Lives: A True Story about Death, Grief and Transformation*. Dianella, Australia: Wilara Press, 2015.

Dawson, Jan Hunt, Ph.D. *Love Only: Lessons from My Near-Death Experiences, Past Life Reviews, and Aftereffects*. Charleston, S.C.: Cardinal Rules Press, 2016.

Estill, Monica. *The Bossy Boulder: How Small Is Big and Big Is Small* (for the kid in all of us). Self-published. ISBN 978-1-59433-385-9. Monica drew all the illustrations, and she has a line of greeting cards. Contact her at monicaestill@gmail.com.

Vellekoop, Holly Fox. Holly has thirteen books on Goodreads, the most favorite being *Stone Haven: Murder along the River*. Some of her other books are: *Encouragers: Those Who Help Others Succeed; The Amazing Adventures of Gramma; Teen Lovers: Murder along the River; Watching Corona: From Our Dimension to Yours; Justice and Revenge; How to Help*

When Parents Grieve. Because she is so prolific, go to her website, Holly Fox Vellekoop, for more information.

OTHER HELPFUL BOOKS
ON SUBJECTS IN THIS STUDY

Blayney, R.A. *Transformation: Life Before Birth, Cosmic Consciousness and Alternate Realities.* Clarington, Ontario, Canada: AbSent Publishing, 2019.

Brandon, Diane B. *Born Aware: Stories & Insights from Those Spiritually Aware Since Birth.* Woodbury, Minn.: Llewellyn Publishers, 2017.

Carman, Elizabeth, and Neil Carman. *Cosmic Cradle.* Berkeley, Calif.: North Atlantic Books, 2013.

Cayce, Hugh Lynn. *Venturing Inward: Safe and Unsafe Ways to Explore the Unconscious Mind.* Original was published in New York by Harper & Row, 1964. Now in continuous publication through the A.R.E. in Virginia Beach, Virginia.

Chambers, John. *The Secret Life of Genius: How 24 Great Men and Women Were Touched by Spiritual Worlds.* Rochester, Vt.: Destiny Books, 2009.

Dyer, Wayne W., M.D., and Dee Garnes. *Memories of Heaven: Children's Astounding Recollections of the Time before They Came to Earth.* Carlsbad, Calif.; Hay House, 2015.

Grof, Stanislav. *Beyond the Brain: Birth, Death, and Transcendence in Psychotherapy.* Albany, N.Y.: SUNY Press, 1985.

Hallett, Elisabeth. *Stories of the Unborn Soul: The Mystery and Delight of Pre-Birth Communication.* Bloomington, Ind.: iUniverse, 2002.

Hinze, Sarah. *Coming from the Light: Spiritual Accounts of Life Before Life.* New York: Simon & Schuster, 1997; *We Lived in Heaven: Spiritual Accounts of Souls Coming to Earth.* Provo, Utah: Spring Creek Book Co., 2006.

Jung, C. G. *The Earth Has a Soul: Nature, Technology & Modern Life.* Berkeley, Calif.; North Atlantic Books, 2002.

McGivern, Patricia Seaver. *Angel Babies: Messages from Miscarried and Other Lost Babies*. Bloomington, Ind.: iUniverse, 2009.

Roger, Bernard. *The Initiatory Path in Fairy Tales: The Alchemical Secrets of Mother Goose*. Rochester, Vt.: Inner Traditions, 2015.

Scheffler, Harlan Carl. *The Quest: Helping Our Children Find Meaning and Purpose*. United Kingdom: George Ronald Pub. Ltd, 2006.

Smith, Mark. *Auras: See Them in Only 60 Seconds*. New Delhi: Pustak Mahal Publisher, 2004. You may want to seriously consider getting this book. Mark Smith had a near-death experience while still in an incubator, weighing three pounds. It happened in an Army Quonset hut nursery. His story, what he remembers, and how he has matured duplicates the stories you have read in this book.

Tucker, Jim B., M.D. *Return to Life: Extraordinary Cases of Children Who Remember Past Lives*. New York: St. Martin's, 2015.

Resources

The following is a list of people and organizations that can provide you with additional information or assistance.

American Center for the Integration of
Spiritually Transformative Experiences (ACISTE)
PO Box 834, Little Elm, TX 75068
Email: info@aciste.org or dina@dinavarano.net

Association for Research and Enlightenment (A.R.E.) (Edgar Cayce)
215 67th Street, Virginia Beach, VA 23451-2061
Phone: 800-333-4499 (U.S. or Canada), 1-757-428-3588
Email: are@edgarcayce.org.
Website: search on Edgar Cayce

Hellinger, Bert (Family Constellations)
Website: search on "Hellinger Institute of Northern California"

Baumgarten, Nancy
Profound Awareness Institute
107 Wild Iris Lane, Hendersonville, NC 28739
Website: search on "Profound Awareness Institute"
Email: nancy@psykids.org.

Chamberlain Communications
909 Hayes Avenue, San Diego, CA 92103
Fax: 619-296-9091
Email: wombpsi@msn.com.

Herrick, Karen
Email: karen@karenherrick.com

Hunt, Valerie V.
Malibu Publishing Co.
PO Box 4234, Malibu, CA 90265

Kramarik, Akiane, described in Gary Noel's article "Artistic Child Genius," can be obtained from the American Federation of Astrologers
6535 South Rural Road, Tempe, AZ 85283
Phone: 480-838-1751

Pennington, Judith
Email: judithpennington@rcn.com

Robinson, Winter
Phone: 207-929-6960
Email: winter@winterrobinson.com
Website: search on "Winter Robinson"

SaintA
8901 W. Capitol Drive
Milwaukee, WI 53222
Phone: 414-463-1880 or 800-840-1880
Website: search on "SaintA"

You can view the television show about SaintA done by Oprah Winfrey on the CBS News website by searching "Oprah Winfrey Treating Childhood Trauma." A screening quiz for post-traumatic stress disorder (PTSD) can be found on the Anxiety and Depression Association of America website.

Silverman, Linda Kreger
Gifted Development Center
8120 Sheridan Blvd., Suite C-111, Westminster, CO 80003
Phone: 303-837-8370
Website: search on "Gifted Development Center"

Twinless Twins Support Group
PO Box 980481 Ypsilanti, MI 48198-0481
Website: search on "Twinless Twins"

University of Science and Philosophy
PO Box 520, Waynesboro, VA 22980
Phone: 800-882-5683 or 540-887-5030
Website: search on "University of Science and Philosophy"
Note: The university is scheduled to open a new headquarters and museum in the spring of 2019. It will be located in Waynesboro, Virginia.

Vazquez, Steven R., Emotional Transformation Therapy (ETT)
Website search on "ETT Center"

Wisnieski, Carol Jean
Phone: 415-864-4663
Email: cwisnies@ccsf.edu

International Association for Near-Death Studies

$\mathcal{F}$or forty-plus years, the International Association for Near-Death Studies (IANDS) has been a nonprofit membership organization driven by volunteer leadership. It focuses most of its resources into providing the highest quality information available about NDE-related subjects. IANDS's purpose is to promote responsible, multidisciplinary exploration of near-death and similar experiences, their effects on people's lives, and their implications for beliefs about life, death, and human purpose. IANDS is devoid of bias toward any religious, cultural, or other personal belief systems. It is the only such membership group in the world.

In addition to maintaining an information-rich website, IANDS offers the following:

- An annual conference to engage experiencers/nonexperiencers, members/nonmembers, in addition to other local events
- A peer-reviewed scholarly journal—*Journal of Near-Death Studies*
- A general interest newsletter—*Vital Signs*
- Various brochures, training materials, CDs, DVDs, and course material for medical, mental, and spiritual healthcare providers, experiencers and their families, and the general public
- Geographically distributed discussion and support groups as well as a global framework for online sharing groups

IANDS serves a broad range of people: experiencers, researchers, healthcare professionals, family and friends of experiencers, educators, and the general public. Contact:

International Association for Near-Death Studies (IANDS)
2741 Campus Walk Avenue, Bldg. 500
Durham, NC 27705
Phone: 919-383-7940
Email: services@iands.org
Website: search on IANDS

Index

Page numbers in *italics* indicate illustrations.

About the Author

*A*fter a long public-service and business career, P. M. H. decided to become a bank manager. In 1977, she was enrolled in classes through the American Banking Institute at the bank where she worked, when she was raped, miscarried, and died three times in three months, each time having an NDE. Complications led to three breakdowns later that year, necessitating that she relearn how to crawl, walk, climb stairs, run, tell the difference between left and right, hear properly, see properly, and rebuild all her belief systems. The "Voice Like None Other," that spoke to her during her third NDE, told her to do the research she is now famous for. She began that work later in 1978, making her one of the early pioneers in near-death research. The book you have just read is her eighteenth—either about the phenomenon or how it affects the people involved.

For information about her many books, published papers, articles, verifications (including one in the *Lancet Medical Journal,* 2001), YouTube videos, blogs, and radio and television shows, go to her website: www.pmhatwater.com.

She produces a free monthly newsletter titled *For the Curious.* Those wishing to subscribe are asked to do so on her website. Now in her 80s, she still travels, gives talks, and invites people to look past appearances for the truth that underlies what they think they know.